Advance Praise

"Tonille Miller has created a critical resource for leaders navigating the future of work. The Flourishing Effect breaks down the barriers between employee well-being and business performance, showing how they are one and the same."

— Brian Elliott, author of How the Future Works and co-founder, Future Forum

"This book is a wake-up call and a roadmap. Miller doesn't just diagnose what's broken—she gives you the tools to fix it."

— Matt Higgins, CEO, RSE Ventures; investor, Shark Tank

"The Flourishing Effect is essential reading for any leader who wants to build an organization that wins—by taking seriously the people who make it run."

— Dorie Clark, Wall Street Journal bestselling author of The Long Game; Duke Fuqua School of Business

"Tonille Miller understands what most organizations still don't: that well-being isn't a perk. It's the foundation of everything."

— Jen Fisher, Human Sustainability Leader; co-author, Work Better Together

"A compelling and practical guide to the future of work. Miller synthesizes the research and brings it to life with stories that stick."

— Bhushan Sethi, Global People and Organization Co-Leader, PwC

"Dave Ulrich has called people your greatest asset. This book shows you how to actually act like it."

— Dave Ulrich, Rensis Likert Professor, University of Michigan; co-founder, the RBL Group

The Flourishing Effect

Unlocking Employee Thriving and High
Performance as Your Competitive Edge

Tonille Miller

Elevate Press

The Flourishing Effect:

Unlocking Employee Thriving and High Performance as Your Competitive Advantage.

Published by Elevate Press, New York, New York.

Library of Congress Cataloging-in-Publication Data is available upon request.

ISBN: 979-8-9887338-5-0 (pbk)

ISBN: 979-8-9887338-1-2 (ebook)

Cover design by LunaDesigns

Cover image by Stefan Pinter

Contents

INTRODUCTION 1

PART 1 9
How We've Been Working Isn't Working

1. 1925 Called; They Want Their Ways of 11
Working Back

2. What Got Us Here Won't Get Us There 19

PART 2 29
How We Fix It

3. The New Deal: An Evolved Social Contract 31

4. Update Your Operating System to Meet the 45
Moment

5. Is Your Culture Driving Strategy or Burning It 65
Down?

6. Give Them Something To Believe In 83

7. The Cheat Code for Engagement 97

8. The King Has Been Dethroned 113

9. The Foundation of High Performance 135

10. Connection and Community 145

11. Treat People Like Adults 153

12. Make Them a Better Version of Themselves   163

13. The Art of Meaning Making   177

14. Your Company IS the Product: The EX   187
    Delivers the CX

15. Sending an Email Isn't Change Management   203

CONCLUSION   227

REFERENCES   233

To my mother,

who has always inspired me to find a better way.

INTRODUCTION

This moment is more significant than most of us have acknowledged. As we emerge from the disruptions of the past several years—a global pandemic, social upheaval, economic uncertainty, a shifting business landscape—we find ourselves at a genuine inflection point.

We've outgrown the old ways of thinking, living, and working, yet are still trying to navigate an unprecedented new world with outdated tools.

In many ways, this moment parallels the dawn of the Italian Renaissance. Fourteenth-century Europe had outgrown its old institutions. The Black Plague killed over a third of the world's population and shattered faith in the Church's authority. Commerce had stalled. Trade, learning, and innovation had ground to a halt.

What emerged from that collapse was not despair—it was a rebirth. People began looking beyond institutions toward community life, human progress, critical thinking, and the exploration of new ideas. The move toward personal agency and the questioning of traditional authority ended the feudal system and put freedom back into the hands of individuals.

Into this moment stepped the Medici family of Florence. Bankers and traders by origin, they recognized the shift in the zeitgeist and decided to operationalize it. They cultivated a dense network of extraordinary writers, scholars, architects, artists, and engineers, branding their effort "an intellectual and artistic revolution." They sponsored Michelangelo, da Vinci, Botticelli.

Attuned to human nature, the Medicis created the conditions for intrinsic motivation and high performance by providing a clear and inspiring purpose, heightened autonomy, creative freedom, a sense of community and belonging, recognition, and genuine investment in people's development.

Cosimo de 'Medici in particular understood that treating artists better meant better work. He recognized, rewarded, and invested in their development. He removed friction and enabled the artists to focus on creating. He leveraged the power of community, giving them a sense of belonging and a way to be part of something larger than themselves by working collectively toward a great mission. The remarkable art and innovations they produced served as powerful symbols of Florence's influence in society—and as catalysts for transforming the world.

Today's leaders and organizations can learn from the Medici playbook. Since the industrial era, organizations have dominated our society, with employees serving as cogs in the machine. But today, we find ourselves in a new world—one of technological advancement, new values, and new expectations—that has rendered the organization an increasingly irrelevant entity, unless it evolves.

As Fortune 500 veteran Alan Murray writes in Tomorrow's Capitalist: My Search for the Soul of Business, fifty years ago, 85% of the value created in companies came from materials the company owned—land, machinery, buildings, equipment. Today, more than 84% of value comes from things like intellectual property, software, and the emotional connection a brand has with its consumers.

These are entirely dependent on people. On human ingenuity, empathy, and critical thinking. People literally are, as professor and management guru Dave Ulrich would say, "your greatest asset." Without them, no organization can create and deliver value to external stakeholders such as customers, investors, and communities.

This shift toward the majority of value coming from people's most human capabilities, coupled with the increasing integration of automation and artificial intelligence, makes it more critical than ever for companies to elicit, cultivate, and harness the most exceptional capabilities of their human workforce to succeed.

Yet most are grappling with a trifecta of a skills shortage, a shrinking labor pool, and an inability to attract, engage, and retain the best talent with conventional approaches.

Contrary to popular memes, this isn't because "no one wants to work anymore." The gig economy and entrepreneurship are booming. The problem stems from work experiences that are full of friction, run counter to human nature, and are disconnected from reality.

Even organizations that manage to attract great talent find themselves inadvertently creating environments where employees feel disengaged or stifled—and as a result, they either languish or leave.

My goal with this book is to shed light on the key areas that hinder your ability to attract, engage, and unleash high performance in your organization, and to show you how to instead, cultivate a distinct competitive edge through your talent. I will arm you with the proof points, guidance, and tools to create the conditions for your people to be the most productive, engaged, and flourishing version of themselves.

So why am I taking you on this journey? Well, from the time I was a little girl, I observed how work dominated most people's lives, and yet it was rare for someone to say they loved what they did. This realization—that most people, as Henry David Thoreau said, "lead lives of quiet desperation"—fueled me to find a better way.

This, and the idea that work seeps into the lives of all of us, exerting its influence on everything from our ability to support our families, our sense of self-worth, our level of vitality, how we treat others, and our overall life satisfaction, has made it my mission to figure out how to create work experiences that not only don't suck people's souls—but actually enrich their lives.

After spending fifteen years as a management consultant, organizational psychologist, and executive coach for large global organizations, high-growth startups, and entrepreneurs, I've discovered what trips leaders and organizations up—and what works. And guess what? The things that enable people to thrive as humans are the exact things that make them perform at the highest levels and deliver real business results.

This playbook will help close the gap between what leaders and the organization are trying to accomplish, and what employees need to do the best work of their lives.

This is an invitation to reimagine work and steward its evolution. Now let's take a spin around what isn't working, and why, so we can fix it and move forward.

This book is structured into 2 parts. Part 1 unpacks how we got here and why work isn't really working for anyone today—the mindsets and practices that, while perhaps effective at one point, no longer align with the needs and expectations of today's organizations, employees, or customers, and why we need to change them.

Part 2 moves into solutions. Each chapter addresses a particular aspect of the organizational experience that's not cutting it today, combining case studies and research with practical tools and easy-to-implement strategies.

Chapter 3 revisits the social contract and explores a better, more evolved partnership. Chapter 4 tackles antiquated workplace practices and how to modernize them. Chapter 5 shows how to leverage culture strategically. Chapter 6 explores how an authentic purpose can serve as a powerful north star. Chapter 7 makes the case for why diversity, equity, inclusion, and belonging are table stakes. Chapter 8 uncovers the fundamental shift in leadership and how today's leaders can adapt.

Chapters 9 – 13 explore how meeting your people's key human needs—well-being, connection, autonomy, growth, mastery, purpose, and meaning—is the best way to increase intrinsic motivation, engagement, performance, and loyalty. Chapter 14 brings it all together into a holistic employee experience designed to deliver your customer experience. And Chapter 15 arms you with the understanding of why most change initiatives fail—and how to drive change in ways people actually want to follow.

PART 1

How We've Been Working Isn't Working

Chapter 1

1925 Called; They Want Their Ways of Working Back

Over time, the employer/employee relationship has been shaped by market forces, expectations, technology, regulations, and the overall business milieu. Prior to recent years, when technology essentially democratized the landscape, organizations were the hub of all activity.

Drawing inspiration from the landlord and indentured servant model, they retained control over customer relationships and means of value creation, such as property, infrastructure, and equipment.

Given the limited proximity, physical mobility, and resources back then, workers heavily relied on the organization as a structure to secure a paycheck in exchange for their labor. Though unions emerged as a powerful force in safeguarding the rights of workers, for the most part, organizations retained the upper hand.

The agricultural worker gave way to artisans and skilled craftsmen, who honed their expertise with pride. They had ownership over how the work was performed and were able to see the impact it had.

The Industrial Age brought a fundamental shift when factories and Henry Ford's mass production model took over. In an attempt to standardize the work as much as possible, Frederick Taylor and his engineering colleagues converted jobs into a series of simplified tasks that could be performed by unskilled, easily trained workers.

The jobs were dumbed down to be more efficient for the organization, separating thinking from doing and making the work as controllable, predictable, and efficient as possible.

According to organizational theorist Lynda Gratton, "In the second Industrial Revolution, engineers redesigned factories to make employees fit into the production line. By doing so, workers lost their autonomy, becoming as interchangeable as the parts they created." The employee was seen as an input to production, where the goal was to get as much consistent, repeatable output as possible.

As renowned psychologist and professor Barry Schwartz points out, unlike machines, humans are incredibly malleable and are heavily influenced by their environment. The institutions in which we live and work design our human nature. So we "design human nature by designing the institutions in which people live and work."

As this occurred and organizations grew larger, the norm shifted towards a hierarchical structure, top-down management, and centralized decision-making, giving rise to bureaucracy, and consequently, employees feeling a diminishing sense of significance and value.

This approach proved somewhat effective in a slower-moving world where only a select few at the top had access to the information required for effective leadership and decision-making.

The 1950s, 1960s, and 1970s witnessed the emergence of the Company Man (it usually was a man), who put the organization before everything else. Employees gave their blood, sweat, and tears to an organization, often for the tenure of their career, and were rewarded with predictable promotions, raises, and a nice pension upon retirement. Leaders used to brag about how much they paid their workers because it signaled the organization's prosperity.

However, when Milton Friedman's doctrine hit the scene in the 1970s, all that changed. Friedman argued that a corporation's greatest responsibility was maximizing profits for shareholders. This inspired a breed of CEO disciples who became laser-focused on short-term gains for shareholders at all costs.

None epitomized this better than Jack Welch, who took over GE in the 1980s. He flipped the switch, treating people as expenses on the balance sheet rather than assets, or humans for that matter.

As David Gelles notes in his book *The Man Who Broke Capitalism: How Jack Welch Gutted the Heartland and Crushed the Soul of Corporate America—and How to Undo His Legacy*, "Welch reshaped the company and the economy, unleashing a series of mass layoffs and factory closures that destabilized the American working class, becoming the first CEO to use downsizing as a tool to improve corporate profitability, and embracing outsourcing and offshoring in an endless quest for cheap labor."

Newsweek aptly coined his new nickname, Neutron Jack, after the Neutron bomb, which "gets rid of the people but leaves the buildings." This focus on short-term profit at employees' expense deteriorated trust and loyalty and established the expendable attitude towards employees that still permeates many organizations today.

Contrary to popular belief, today's younger workforce is not a bunch of lazy, entitled job hoppers. Instead, they are intelligent agents following the principles of behavioral economics.

Take the Millennials, for instance, who entered the workforce during the tumultuous times of the Great Recession, when most organizations were cutting costs and lowering salaries. According to billionaire and Coalition for Inclusive Capitalism founder Lynn Forester de Rothschild, between 2020 and 1982, wages increased by 70%, whereas the stock market grew by 400%. However, between 1980 and 2020, wages only increased by 15%, while the stock market saw an astounding 800% growth.

Under these circumstances, today's younger workforce had no choice but to take on lower-paying jobs to make ends meet and repay their student loans. Consequently, the most promising way for them to secure a promotion or salary increase was (and still is) to switch to another company. They have acted precisely in line with the incentives of the system.

Despite leaders' bemoaning the idea that employee loyalty no longer exists, today's workforce is not willing to stake their futures on an organization that fails to offer them the security, fair treatment, and adequate wages enjoyed by previous generations.

Today, there are no pensions, wages are underwhelming, and companies are perfectly comfortable laying off staff as soon as their profits dip below a certain margin.

Many organizations have left people feeling dispensable, forcing them to search for other ways to secure their financial future.

A recent Deloitte study found 26% of Gen Z and 8% of Millennials are working a second job due to financial stress. Two-thirds of workers say that recent waves of layoffs have eroded their trust in the security of full-time employment. 52% of knowledge workers hesitate to commit to one employer anymore. As reported by Harvard Business Review, 67% of independent workers feel more secure working for themselves than for a single employer.

At the same time, technological advancements have leveled the playing field, providing new opportunities and reducing barriers to entry. Individuals are now able to create value without being restricted to a particular company, job, or location. They are no longer reliant on traditional organizational structures for employment or income.

For today's workforce, the solution is to embrace side hustles, gig portfolios, multiple income streams, and entrepreneurship—all providing more stability and opportunities to leverage their full range of skills, while growing their network and income. More than half of the workforce is expected to be freelance by 2027.

To avoid being left in the lurch, organizations will need to provide their people with something this new marketplace of opportunities can't offer.

This isn't a threat to organizations—it's a wake-up call and an opportunity. Companies that adapt their models, their cultures, and their value propositions to compete in this new landscape will attract extraordinary talent. Those that don't will find themselves outcompeted not just by rival firms, but by the freelance economy, the gig economy, and the entrepreneurial ecosystem they helped create by failing to retain their best people.

The organizations that win the next decade of talent will be the ones that offer something no marketplace can: a sense of belonging, meaningful work, genuine development, and a culture where people feel seen and valued.

Chapter 2

What Got Us Here Won't Get Us There

Industrial-era workplace practices and mindsets may have worked for a time, but gradually these ways of working, designed for maximum efficiency, surveillance, and compliance of an unthinking workforce, have become obsolete.

With globalization, advancements in technology, and unprecedented volatility, almost everything around us has changed. And yet, the way we work has largely remained stagnant.

As the workforce and world have undergone significant transformation, particularly coming out of the pandemic, most organizations haven't updated their structures, norms, technologies, management practices, social contracts, and overall employee experience to keep pace.

The impact can be seen in our current epidemic of burnout, turnover, disengagement, and low satisfaction at work. As Jon Clifton, CEO of Gallup, explains, "Humanity is trying to figure out every way possible to get away from work. Employees aren't just emotionally detached—they're angry about what's happening in their workplace."

According to the 2023 Gallup State of the Global Workplace Report, 59% of employees are disengaged, and this epidemic comes with a hefty price tag. Disengagement costs organizations nearly nine trillion dollars annually, a staggering 9% of each disengaged employee's salary, while attrition costs another trillion dollars annually.

When you add the $8.8 trillion cost of lost productivity due to disengaged employees, we're talking about 9% of the global GDP—nearly double the market cap of Google, Amazon, and Apple combined. And that doesn't even account for the time, energy, and life stolen from each disengaged employee.

While the benefits of engaging employees and activating high performance are well understood, the lack of these is often positioned as a problem on the employee's side. Leaders frequently ask, "Why aren't my people engaged?" rather than looking at how their own behavior, the company's culture, or ways of working directly impact engagement.

People don't choose to disengage from work. No one wakes up and decides they want to spend most of their waking hours in a state of boredom, frustration, anxiety, stress, or alienation just to earn a paycheck.

Disengagement is a coping mechanism any healthy human would employ to avoid the cognitive dissonance, or mental discomfort of having to function in an environment where they find themselves unsafe, stifled, or in otherwise warped experiences of reality.

Let that sink in. People disengage or disconnect psychologically to remove themselves, at least mentally, from experiences where they feel a lack of belonging, agency, stimulation, purpose, or connection to reality.

Unfortunately, many organizations create these exact experiences. Let's examine some of them up close.

The Organization Provides a Distorted Reality

Trying to use old formulas in a new reality produces a distorted experience for people. And to be clear, we are in a new reality. Organizations that still operate from old assumptions, mindsets, and ways of working are that much easier to disrupt because they become increasingly irrelevant to their employees and customers.

It Feels Like 1985 at Work

The majority of today's workforce is accustomed to frictionless, personalized experiences and consumer grade technology in their personal life. Yet, many organizations still use clunky technology and don't effectively leverage data and AI to personalize the experience. This makes your employees have to step back in time to go to work.

This is especially problematic for Digital Natives (born after 1980), whose lives revolve primarily around digital interactions, with analog experiences being secondary. Simply carrying out their tasks within your organization feels disorienting and like an extra layer of work.

Operating From an Outdated Social Contract

Unfortunately, the old social contract between employer and employee is no longer valid. Yesterday's promise of security and prosperity in exchange for career-long loyalty has become today's inadequate compensation, frequent layoffs, and portfolio careers.

The workforce has learned that organizations are not coming to save them, and as a result, they are no longer willing to devote themselves to any one company based on false promises. In Chapter 3, we'll explore a better way.

Work Practices That Contradict Human Nature

Many of the ways organizations operate stifle employees' human needs for autonomy, growth, agency, certainty, mastery, and meaning, and as a result, reduce engagement and performance.

Treating People Like Value to Be Extracted

Over the years, we have increasingly tried to extract as much as possible from employees in a relentless pursuit of productivity. As Seth Godin emphasizes in his latest book, *The Song of Significance*, this leads to harmful competition where companies constantly strive for lower costs and higher efficiency, ultimately resulting in a race to the bottom.

Treating humans transactionally, like machines tends to produce resentfulness and giving the bare minimum until they leave. Leading them with generosity, on the other hand, induces the psychological principle of reciprocity and the desire to go above and beyond.

The Work Itself Isn't Engaging

For a significant number of employees, the work they do isn't engaging because, as we discussed in Chapter 1, it has been stripped of autonomy, creativity, and individual ownership in return for standardization and consistency.

Unfortunately, much of our current work is still rooted in the Taylorized factory model, where work tasks were mechanized and devoid of personal agency.

This produced employees who, in the words of Adam Smith, "became as stupid and ignorant as it is possible for a human creature to become." This left workers feeling empty and devoid of any real satisfaction from their work.

This is like a slow, painful death to today's knowledge worker who is more educated than previous generations and craves growth, interesting problems to solve, and progression. A dearth of those things creates boredom and makes people ready to walk.

Bad Managers

There are mountains of data showing people don't quit jobs—they quit bosses. Gallup research shows how crucial great management is—with 70% of employee engagement attributed to the manager and $360 billion in losses from bad leadership each year.

In Chapter 8 we'll take a closer look at the primary factors perpetuating ineffective managers and shed light on what leaders can do to up their game to lead in this new world.

Treating Adults Like Children

How about when employees are subjected to micromanagement, surveillance, or compelled to adhere to arbitrary office attendance requirements as a way to validate their productivity? During the pandemic, there was a 50% uptick in surveillance software purchased.

Plenty of studies over the past few years have shown this leads to learned helplessness, increased stress, and turnover, and even makes workers do their job worse on purpose.

And how many people feel they have to sneak out of the office to attend to personal matters such as doctor appointments or picking up their children from school? In Chapter 11, I'll show you how to avoid this costly mistake and instead foster an environment of motivation, agility, and ownership.

Lack Of Clarity and Direction

Gallup research shows only half of employees know what is expected of them at work. Beyond the turnover and anxiety this produces for employees, leaders need to ask themselves: how are their people supposed to deliver on the strategy if they don't know what it is?

In today's rapidly changing and uncertain environment, everyone in the organization must have a clear understanding of what needs to be achieved and be empowered to take ownership and make decisions.

However, in many organizations, there isn't visibility around the direction and purpose, or an explanation of how employees fit into the bigger picture.

Not Giving Employees a Say

When people aren't included in decisions impacting their job, they will not buy in. I see this often when organizations make changes without involving the workforce in the design and implementation of solutions, and then they wonder why they see resistance and poor adoption rates.

Most of today's workforce has grown up in collaboration with their parents, teachers, and even brands. As a result, they expect to be asked for their perspective and have a dialogue around their experiences.

Superhuman Expectations

With companies increasingly trying to do more with less, expectations of employees have progressed significantly from the 40-hour workweek of mindless labor of previous eras. However, they have failed to recognize that pushing employees to work faster and harder only goes so far. There is a limit to how much productivity can be squeezed out of a human workforce.

Today's expectation is for employees to be always-on, bringing their highest capabilities to go above and beyond as the baseline every day. It's clear from the skyrocketing rates of burnout and turnover that this is no longer working.

Not Having An Employee-Centric Lens

One of the key tenets of behavioral economics and persuasion psychology is to make it as easy as possible for people to do what you want them to do. This is the opposite of how most organizations operate.

It Feels Like an Extra Job on Top Of Their Job

As technology implementations and other changes become more and more prevalent, employees encounter increasing amounts of friction when trying to adopt them. This environment is ripe for burnout and disengagement.

The organization is the interface employees use to deliver your brand to the market. The primary focus should be on making it as effortless and energizing as possible for people to do their best work and deliver value to customers. Chapter 14 will guide you in removing these sources of friction.

The Organization's Leaders Are the Stars

As the organization grows larger, each individual employee feels smaller. If your onboarding, town halls, and other interactions are all about the company or the leadership team, it makes employees feel like just a number. This quickly decreases their feelings of agency and motivation to go above and beyond. Chapter 14 will show you how to take an employee-centric perspective in designing every touchpoint.

The Environment Isn't Inclusive

As the workforce has become more diverse, one would assume feelings of belonging would grow, but the contrary has happened.

Today's workforce looks very different from the white, cisgender, analog men our workplaces were built by and for. Yet, current workplace norms are still largely based on masculine defaults and white professional standards of the "Mad Men" era. This worker didn't need to juggle his job with caregiving and domestic duties because he had someone at home whose sole job was to care for him, the home, and the children. This means he was able to put in plenty of face time and attend after-hours events.

The reality today's average employee faces is far from this. In Chapter 7, we'll look at how to overcome this and create an inclusive environment where everyone can bring the best of themselves.

The good news is that every single one of these blind spots is fixable. None of them require a revolution—they require intention.

The organizations that move fastest are the ones whose leaders are willing to look honestly at the experience they're creating and ask hard questions: Is this the kind of place where I would want to spend forty or fifty hours a week? Does this environment bring out the best in people, or does it suppress it? Is the friction I'm creating necessary—or just a legacy of how we've always done things? If you can hold those questions honestly, the path forward becomes much clearer.

Now that we've shined a light on how we got here and why it's no longer working, how do we move forward? Let's start with revisiting the social contract, and changing the very foundation upon which everything else is built.

PART 2

How We Fix It

Chapter 3

The New Deal: An Evolved Social Contract

How it must feel as a newly-minted employee who's initially embraced as a valued member of the "family," to later face the company's decision to let them go as part of a cost-cutting measure.

Picture this: you've worked for one of the very profitable Silicon Valley tech giants for over fifteen years and wake up one day to discover your work email account deactivated.

This was how Jenny, a former employee, learned she was part of a recent mass layoff. She then joined many of her former colleagues to share the news on LinkedIn and vent about the betrayal and lack of loyalty. Not a good look for the company.

The implications of layoffs go beyond the damage to employees who are asked to leave. It impacts the brand to prospective employees and customers. It also produces scar tissue for everyone who remains, in the form of survivor guilt, hypervigilance, and decreased performance while the focus shifts to looking for work.

Survivors have a 41% decline in job satisfaction, a 20% decline in organizational commitment, and a 36% decline in performance. Harvard Business Review shows even a 1% layoff can create a 31% voluntary attrition spike.

I get it; sometimes layoffs are the only way for the business to survive, but become problematic when they're not handled strategically and humanely.

Consider two layoffs; two very different philosophies.

When the pandemic erased 80% of Airbnb's business overnight in 2020, CEO Brian Chesky put on a masterclass in how to let people go with dignity. When Elon Musk acquired Twitter in 2022 and needed to service $13.2 billion in acquisition debt, he demonstrated the opposite.

Chesky's letter to departing employees is worth studying — it should be required reading in every MBA program. He opened by taking full responsibility, walking employees through the data and reasoning behind the decision with transparency rather than corporate euphemism. He acknowledged the human cost plainly, without deflection. The tone was genuine, not managed messaging.

Departing employees received generous severance, extended benefits, outplacement support, a talent directory to help them land elsewhere, and they kept their laptops. Small, yet telling gestures.

Perhaps most importantly, Chesky went out of his way to destigmatize the cuts entirely. The layoffs, he made clear, reflected the state of the world — not the quality of the people leaving. That distinction mattered. It protected the dignity of those let go, and it told the people who remained exactly what kind of leader they were working for.

Let's juxtapose this against the condemnatory layoffs made by Elon Musk soon after he bought Twitter. Some Twitter employees were laid off via email, while others found out by being locked out of work laptops in lieu of an official notice.

No closure. No goodbye. No recognition that what they had given actually mattered. In addition to blaming employees for the company's problems, Musk didn't explain why the layoffs were necessary. Months later, many employees still hadn't received the severance promised.

Update The Social Contract

It's safe to say we've long outgrown the traditional employer-employee relationship in which the job interview was likened to a first date, followed by a blind promise of lifelong loyalty that neither party is likely to uphold.

I propose a new social contract based on transparency, mutual value creation, and a long-term partnership. Consider it an ongoing courtship, with both parties opting in—perhaps every month, just like our favorite subscription services.

This level of expectation-setting, and conscious coupling and uncoupling reduces the likelihood of being caught off guard and enables real-time adjustments based on the employee-employer dynamic and business landscape.

It's a generative partnership requiring maturity from both sides. It focuses on optimizing time, resources, and purpose to add value for both parties and create wins instead of power games based on ego and control.

According to LinkedIn founder Reid Hoffman, organizations should view their talent as allies on a tour of duty. While employees won't stay forever, they can continue to assist the organization long after they leave. Success in this paradigm requires organizations to take the long view, lead with generosity, and be intentional about onboarding and offboarding talent.

To orchestrate this shift, organizations must ensure mechanisms for both parties to access and add value quickly and continue to positively impact each other's ecosystem even when not formally engaged. Intelligent organizations understand that today's employee could be tomorrow's client, brand ambassador, talent referrer, or even a boomerang employee.

At LinkedIn, for example, employees are asked at the beginning, what they want to do once they leave. This level of candor allows them to reverse engineer the time spent in the company to be high-impact.

A powerful way for an organization to extend the relationship beyond their time with it is through a comprehensive offboarding program (we'll get more into what this looks like in Chapter 14). By maintaining relationships with former employees, organizations can showcase their commitment to their people and strengthen their reputation in the market.

Throughout my experience, I've observed numerous other untapped sources of value that both the organization and its employees can provide each other. Let's explore some of these new sources of value.

New Sources of Value

There are many no-to-low-cost value streams companies can offer people, beyond standard pay and benefits.

Understand The Job They Hired Their Job to Do

Clayton Christensen had a simple but reframing idea: people don't buy products, they hire them — to accomplish something, solve something, or avoid something.

His classic example involved trying to boost milkshake sales at a fast-food restaurant. Extensive consumer research into flavors, price, and texture yielded nothing. Sales didn't budge. So the team changed the question entirely, asking customers what job they "hired the milkshake to do."

The answer was surprisingly human: most buyers faced a long, boring commute and needed something to make the drive bearable — not necessarily because they were hungry, but because a milkshake fit neatly in a cupholder and kept one hand free for the wheel. That single reframe unlocked the insights that actually moved the needle.

Global Head of People Ops Excellence at Google Bart Linsley has applied this insight to ask thousands of people what job they hire their job to do. He found that for some, it's puzzles to solve; for others, it's status, somewhere to go, enjoyment of the actual tasks, and even feeling useful.

Taking this employee-centric lens enables us to build the employee value proposition more insightfully around what people are actually seeking from their job, not just what the organization thinks will motivate them. This question could easily be asked during onboarding, one-on-ones with managers, employee surveys, and performance reviews.

Organizations that understand how their people think about work and what "job they hire it to do" can position it as a way for employees to achieve their personal goals.

Provide Interesting Problems to Solve

People don't stay with your organization for free lunch and dry cleaning. They stay for the opportunity to solve important problems and be part of something exciting.

A great illustration of this is Paul Starrett, whose team built the Empire State Building in only 13 months. Accomplishing this extraordinary feat in 1930 meant disassembling the Waldorf-Astoria hotel, removing thousands of truckloads of rubble, and designing, constructing, and topping out the new building with interiors.

How did he do it? In addition to providing working conditions the workers said were important, he also positioned the project as a big problem to solve. He asked for ideas from his whole crew.

As a result, creativity poured out. Workers suggested building a mini railway line to transport bricks into the site instead of stacking them on wheelbarrows to be pushed along wobbling wooden gangplanks. Electricians developed wired signaling systems to replace the usual bell ropes to announce when a shipment was coming.

As the various teams worked together in this environment, they found that they could contribute and depend on each other. Starrett was spared the usual high turnover on such construction sites.

Let Them Build It With You

Positioning work as interesting problems to solve co-creatively is a win-win. Employees are more satisfied, engaged, and productive. Organizations get more innovation, better customer service, and lower turnover.

Co-creation is rooted in the belief that the people closest to a challenge often hold the best solutions. Rather than top-down mandates, it invites active participation, collective intelligence, and shared ownership. Teams test, fail, and iterate toward a better solution than any individual could have built alone, and because they helped build it, they're invested in making it work.

Companies can formalized this through cross-functional Tiger Teams or Tour of Duty programs, where employees sign up for 6–18 month projects tackling real business problems.

What makes co-creation so powerful is what psychologists call psychological ownership — the feeling that something is mine, not by legal title, but by active contribution. When employees help shape the strategy, culture, and solutions, they stop being spectators and become stakeholders. Compliance becomes commitment. And the solutions that emerge are not only more innovative — because they draw on more perspectives — but more durable, because the people who must implement them helped design them.

Meet Their Human Needs

People have deep-seated needs for meaning, purpose, esteem, connection, inclusion, and growth. Environments that stifle these needs, impede motivation, engagement, wellbeing, and performance.

Imagine the power of organizations that not only didn't *neglect* these needs, but *met* them.

Today's workers are less rooted in the religious and community institutions that anchored previous generations, and many are reaching traditional life milestones — marriage, family — later, if at all.

That, and the fact that work has become a central tenet of most people's identity, means they are looking for work to meet needs previously met by institutions like marriage, religion, and community. The workplace offers a perfect structure to do this while contributing to business goals.

In her book *Work Pray Code: When Work Becomes Religion in Silicon Valley,* Carolyn Chen tells the story of a devout tech worker who gradually stopped going to church after moving to Silicon Valley. His belief in God hadn't changed. But work was now meeting the same deep needs that church once had — belonging, meaning, purpose.

I'm not saying organizations should lure their people from their religious or community affiliations. But, companies that prioritize meeting the fundamental human needs of their employees in the flow of work are poised to reap substantial benefits, including a more productive and engaged workforce.

Make Them More Valuable in the Marketplace

As workplace expert Heather McGowan argues, learning is the new pension. Not only does today's social contract no longer reward employee loyalty with a pension, but more importantly, learning is how people create their future value. By learning today, they are more valuable tomorrow.

Pew Research showed one of the top reasons people left their jobs during "The Great Resignation" was a lack of growth opportunities. This continues today.

Organizations must realize that growing and developing people isn't just a force multiplier for the business but is an actual currency they can offer employees. In Chapter 12, we'll discuss the many no/low-cost ways to do this.

Untapped Potential

Most organizations never fully tap the skills and potential sitting right inside their workforce — and it's costing them.

Brand Advocacy

In today's hyper-connected world, the boundaries between candidates, employees, customers, and brand advocates have all but dissolved. Your next referral partner, client, or ambassador may already be on your payroll — or interviewing for a job. Yet too many organizations fail to recognize, let alone cultivate, this opportunity.

When I worked at PwC, I was also an adjunct professor at several New York City colleges — which meant I was building PwC's brand on those campuses every time I walked into a classroom. Because PwC invested in my growth, I've never stopped advocating for them. I mention them in media interviews, client conversations, and mentoring sessions. I've referenced them throughout this book. That's not loyalty you can buy with a polished ad campaign — it's loyalty you earn.

Which raises the question: why spend a fortune on stock photos and fabricated narratives when your employees' authentic voices are far more persuasive? Today's candidates and customers are allergic to corporate messaging. What they trust is a genuine glimpse into what it's actually like to work there, told by the people who actually work there.

This only works if your people are proud to be associated with you. Unlike previous generations, today's workforce has carefully built their personal brands, and they're acutely aware of what their affiliations signal online. They won't champion companies that don't reflect their values.

The most compelling employee value propositions don't come from marketing departments. They come from real people sharing real experiences. Equip your employees with simple tools to share day-in-the-life content and you'll have, as Gen Z authority Hannah Grady Williams puts it "an army of authentic recruiters that the younger generation trusts more than traditional ones." All it takes is to have a simple internal channel to quickly greenlight employee-created content — so it can be posted, reshared, and amplified.

The cautionary tale is Sherwin-Williams. When employee Tony Piloseno built a TikTok following of 1.2 million fans by filming himself mixing paint at work, his manager loved it. Corporate marketing did not — and fired him. In doing so, Sherwin-Williams didn't just lose an employee. They handed a competitor 1.2 million engaged followers, along with the customers and future hires who came with them.

Innovation

Some of the most valuable innovation doesn't come from the top of the organization; it comes from the people closest to the work. Involving employees in designing solutions, improving processes, and developing new products doesn't just generate better ideas; it generates commitment to seeing them through.

But this requires the right conditions. Psychologically safe, inclusive environments — where people from different backgrounds feel genuinely heard — are what allow diverse perspectives to surface and collide in productive ways..

Advisory boards and staff councils are particularly effective for stress-testing ideas before they scale, offering leadership a representative read on how changes will land across the organization. More importantly, they signal that input is valued; not just tolerated.

When working with clients facing organizational change, I always recommend bringing potential skeptics into the process early. Asking the people most likely to resist a new initiative to help shape it is one of the most disarming, and effective moves a leader can make. Resistance tends to dissolve when people feel ownership over the outcome.

One client has taken this to scale with a company-wide innovation platform where employees submit ideas for improving products, processes, and ways of working. Leadership reviews submissions, acts on the strongest ones, and publicly credits the people behind them. The result: several new products brought to market, and a workforce that knows their ideas don't disappear into a void.

Intel

In today's rapidly changing world, it's more important than ever for leaders to stay connected to their employees and customers. However, it's increasingly common for senior leaders to be disconnected due to limited digital fluency and, often, very different lived experiences.

According to Gartner, only 12% of leaders have the digital agility to succeed in the future. One way organizations can bridge this gap is by implementing a reverse mentoring program that pairs Digital Natives with senior leaders. These young, tech-savvy employees can offer valuable insights into the digital landscape and help leaders stay up to date with the latest trends and technologies.

I had a client recently who appointed a Digital Native employee, along with leaders of their employee resource groups, to serve on the leadership team. These employees were able to offer a fresh perspective and highlight blind spots that senior leaders may miss. One of their first projects was updating the benefits program to be more relevant to their diverse employee population. These folks provided feedback on the current program and ideas on how to make it more inclusive.

The organization found that over half of the employees would even take a pay cut if they were offered more personalized benefits. The new benefits program that resulted was more like a menu of options employees could choose from based on their needs. This resulted in a 30% increase in satisfaction with the company's benefits offerings and an overall engagement bump of 1%.

This is just one example of the intelligence and innovation that lies untapped when organizations treat employees purely as a means to an end.

When you genuinely listen to your people, when you give them a real seat at the table and the authority to act on what they know, the ROI compounds in ways that are difficult to manufacture from the top down.

The question every leader should be asking is not just 'What can we offer our employees?' but 'What can our employees offer us—and what conditions do we need to create to unlock that?'

The answer to that second question is the foundation of a truly competitive talent strategy.

Chapter 4

Update Your Operating System to Meet the Moment

Most organizations still operate from antiquated, industrial-era models of how a workplace looks and functions. These century-old constructs formulated on factory floors served a purpose when the speed of supervised, repetitive, mindless output was the goal.

However, over the years, the desired aim of the human worker has radically shifted from mimicking a machine toward leveraging its full humanness and higher capabilities. In this chapter, we'll explore outdated workplace practices in desperate need of disruption, and show you how to bring them into the future.

Work Is Something We Do, Not a Place We Go

As someone who has worked equally successfully remotely, in-office, and hybrid for over a decade, I can definitively say we're making way too big a deal of the current RTO debate. Remote, hybrid, and distributed work is not new.

Any sales team, consulting firm, or organization with more than one office has been working this way for decades. And because today's world relies so heavily on technology, most things are done virtually, even when people are in the office.

The pandemic provided the perfect catalyst for the world to demonstrate, at scale, that work can and does happen outside of a particular place.

Although the conditions of our forced distributed work experiment were suboptimal, numerous silver linings have emerged for us to consider as we design a better future of work.

While the pandemic forced many organizations to adopt remote work, it also had surprising positive impacts on workplace equity and culture.

It made it easier to identify and address inequities such as microaggressions, code-switching, and emotional labor. The data shows underrepresented groups benefit significantly from remote work.

Future Forum reported a 51% increase in a sense of workplace belonging for Black workers and a 64% increase in their ability to manage stress when working from home. Additionally, 83% of Black respondents preferred working fully remote or hybrid, while over 43% of women preferred working mostly remotely because of its flexibility.

The data also shows fully remote knowledge workers report the highest levels of overall satisfaction, and 35% of people even reported that remote work improved their organizational culture because they were trusted and treated like adults.

While some leaders worry that remote work could decrease collaboration and innovation, Stanford professor Jeremy Utley suggests that distributed work can increase creativity.

Utley, the author of the new book *Ideaflow*, believes the key to fostering innovative ideas is to have as many sources of different and disparate input as possible. And guess what? Having everyone in the same conference room, at the same time, with the same experience is the opposite of that.

Remote work enables organizations to tap into a larger, more diverse, cost-effective talent pool while shrinking expensive, carbon-heavy real estate footprints.

It behooves leaders to recognize the benefits of it as a long-term strategy to create a more equitable, innovative, and sustainable workplace.

A year after launching its "Live and Work Anywhere" policy for employees, Airbnb has seen increased employee satisfaction and diversity, as well as lower attrition. All while revenue has grown 70%.

How to Work Hybrid / Distributed Successfully

Upskill leaders. Many leaders have struggled to adapt with the shift toward remote and hybrid work models. The traditional command and control methods that once yielded success are no longer effective in this new reality.

As a result, many leaders find themselves floundering in unfamiliar territory. It's particularly unsetting when combined with the potential threat to their status and positional power. It's not uncommon for leaders to feel disoriented or even a loss of purpose when they can't rely on having their employees around them.

Many are unsure of how to lead or manage their teams in this new world. But there is a wealth of resources, including coaching, courses, and other content available to help leaders upskill and adapt to this new reality.

While important in any environment, here are several key tenets of successful leadership at a distance:

Clarity: Make the implicit explicit. Successful remote leaders clearly communicate goals, deadlines, and performance expectations to staff, ensuring everyone is on the same page. Setting team agreements and sharing preferred communication styles is helpful too.

Trust and Autonomy: If you don't trust your people, ask yourself why you hired them. Real autonomy means giving people the authority to make decisions and own their work — not just the responsibility without the power.

Managing By Outcomes: Managing by outcomes is a skill that takes practice — and for many leaders, it requires a genuine mindset shift. Start by sitting down with each team member to define what success looks like and how you'll measure it. Clarity upfront removes ambiguity later.

Regular Communication: Effective remote leaders maintain regular and consistent communication with their team members. They utilize various communication channels (videoconferences, emails, and instant messaging) to stay connected and provide guidance.

Extreme Transparency and Listening. Whether your team works remotely, in-office, or somewhere in between, keeping people informed and connected is an ongoing conversation. It should be a two-way dialogue, not a broadcast, embracing multimedia formats like podcasts, videos, and interactive forums to reach people in ways that actually resonate.

Feedback mechanisms — the channels that let employees respond, push back, and be heard — are what transform communication into genuine dialogue. This matters everywhere, but it's especially critical in remote and hybrid environments, where distance can quietly muffle the voices most worth hearing.

Leverage Asynchronous Work and Tools: Invest in collaboration tools that enable seamless idea-sharing and workflow visibility. Use asynchronous tools like email, shared documents, and voice or video messaging to keep everyone informed regardless of location, and use synchronous communication like calls, video meetings, live chat for relationship-building and decisions that benefit from real-time dialogue.

GitLab is the gold standard for remote work done right. The software company has been 100% remote since day one, went public in 2021 at a valuation over $8 billion, and maintains a 90% employee satisfaction rate. They attribute this to two disciplines: asynchronous-first communication and impeccable documentation.

According to Head of Remote Darren Murph, most workplace coms can and should be asynchronous (short videos, voice memos, shared documents) with synchronous time reserved for 1-on-1s and culture-building. GitLab has codified this approach in an open-source remote work playbook available to any organization looking to make the transition.

Leading organizations are already pushing further, using augmented reality, virtual reality, and spatial computing to create remote experiences that feel genuinely immersive. The applications span onboarding, learning and development, and culture-building.

BMW uses a 3D metaverse platform to let global teams collaboratively design and reconfigure factories in real time, eliminating the need for travel. Accenture onboarded over 100,000 people through the metaverse in 2022 alone.

Ensure Development Is a Priority: During the pandemic, I worked with a major bank that had long insisted its apprenticeship model only worked in person. Necessity proved otherwise. Senior employees began copying junior staff on emails and including them in client calls and Zoom meetings — turning everyday interactions into low-stakes learning opportunities. Junior team members brought their questions and observations to weekly one-on-ones, creating a natural feedback loop between exposure and reflection.

The results surprised even the skeptics. Not only did junior employees develop faster, but the model proved more equitable than its in-person predecessor — mentorship was no longer contingent on physical proximity or the confidence to approach a senior leader in the hallway. Access, it turned out, had always been the real barrier.

Equity: Equitable experiences for all employees, regardless of location, should be a design principle, not an afterthought.

When the gap between on-site and remote experience widens, resentment follows. The fix starts with clarity: audit all roles and establish objective criteria for which positions require on-site presence and which don't.

Promotion trends deserve the same scrutiny; proximity bias is real, and the data usually shows it. Every policy, technology platform, and meeting practice should be stress-tested through three lenses: how does this work for someone on-site, hybrid, and fully remote? If the answer isn't "equally well," it needs rethinking.

Default to High-Trust: Don't fall prey to "Productivity Paranoia." Surveillance, monitoring, and micromanagement are canceled. The pandemic prompted many organizations to turn to surveillance software to monitor employees' keystrokes and mouse clicks, eroding trust, morale, and productivity.

Future-of-work experts Heidi Gardner and Mark Mortensen assert that monitoring employees' face time, keystrokes, and hours worked undermines trust, which is critical to building successful teams.

Trust is reciprocal—leaders who prioritize trust and empower their employees with flexibility and autonomy see a virtuous cycle of trust and performance.

By contrast, leaders who cling to outdated command-and-control measures risk a "Zoom Loop" of meaningless monitoring that erodes trust and drives away top talent.

More Accurate Measures of Productivity and Impact: Just as productivity is no longer demonstrated through the number of hours standing on the factory floor, it is not reflected in the number of hours sitting in an office or on a Zoom call. "Productivity has always been a good way to measure the impact of machines; it's just never been a good way to measure the impact of humans," says Atlassian's Work Futurist, Dominic Price.

I always chuckle at leaders who think their highest-performing people are the ones who spend the most time in the office. Here's a hint: They aren't working the entire time. As Parkinson's law states, the work will expand to fill the time allotted for completion.

Because many leaders value face time and expect people to be in the office an arbitrary number of hours per day, people find ways to fill the time—long lunches, online shopping, social media, making four Starbucks runs a day, and desk-bombing others, which actually prevents them from getting focused work done.

All of this speaks to the larger problem of poor proxies of productivity, which rely on visibility (who is spending long hours at the office) and lazy management.

To save your people the boredom and frustration of what journalist Anne Helen Petersen calls LARPing (live-action role-playing) their jobs, let's move toward more accurate measures of performance and impact. The rest is just productivity theater.

One of my favorite innovative companies, CultureRx, was founded by former Best Buy execs Cali Ressler and Jody Thompson. Cali and Jody created a culture transformation methodology called Results-Only Work Environment (ROWE), which ensures leadership focuses on outcomes versus time at the office or physical presence.

In this system, employees are autonomous and have complete control over when, where, and how they work. They are held accountable for clearly defined outcomes, not time spent in an office. Managers and employees partner to clarify the work that needs to be done and how it will be measured. That's it; the what is managed, not how or where.

The ROWE model also has a profound effect on the culture more broadly. When managers stop equating time spent at a desk with contribution, they are forced to develop more sophisticated ways of understanding what people actually produce—and more honest conversations about expectations.

Employees, in turn, stop performing the theater of busyness and start focusing on what genuinely matters. The result is a culture of clarity, ownership, and trust that creates the conditions for people to do the best work of their lives.

Regardless of where, when, or how the work gets done, it's key to align metrics, KPIs, and incentives around outputs instead of inputs. As Brian Elliott, co-founder of Future Forum and a former executive at Slack and Google, notes, when you base your success measures on inputs and outputs, you get quantity, emails, meetings, and potentially arbitrary activity. But activity doesn't equal quality or impact and can even counter results.

Measuring outcomes, however, encourages focus on what matters and an ownership mindset. Employees don't need to work a certain set of hours, so long as they meet their performance metrics. Conducting weekly one-on-ones to review priorities and commitments makes it easy to intervene when progress is lagging.

Getting People Back to Offices

Having said all this, if your organization still absolutely feels it's necessary to get employees back into offices, you'll need to overcome three powerful psychological tensions at play and employ a magnet, not mandate approach.

I think we've all learned from the unsuccessful attempts of leaders who have tried to force employees to return to the office. These mandates fail due to tension of three psychological principles: reactance, loss aversion, and gaslighting.

Reactance emerges when people feel their autonomy is threatened or constrained. In this situation, where leaders make demands of a grown adult—even if it's something the person was already planning to do—the demand itself triggers the person's inner rebel. They feel a strong urge to resist or reject the mandate.

Loss Aversion is a cognitive bias that says the pain of losing something is psychologically twice as powerful as the pleasure of gaining it. During the pandemic, employees were finally treated like adults and allowed to manage when, where, and how they worked. Organizations that attempt to take that freedom away post-pandemic are triggering this pain.

Gaslighting dismisses the reality of what we've collectively experienced during the pandemic. Despite three years of data showing that we can work better, more productively, and happier remotely, many leaders still don't trust their people to work outside the office. It's impossible to go "back to normal."

Force-fitting everyone back into an old, broken model just because it makes a few leaders more comfortable is not the way to go. Organizations that ignore the lessons learned and the reality we now find ourselves in are that much easier to disrupt—because plenty of organizations are moving forward, integrating what they've learned into a better future.

Instead of issuing demands or commands, organizations can be more effective by providing compelling options and allowing room for creativity and experimentation.

Here are some great ways to get started:

Provide Certainty With Organized Hybrid: A top complaint from employees returning to the office is arriving to spend the day on Zoom calls with people in other locations. The commute, it turns out, wasn't worth it.

Organizations can solve this by taking a cue from the appointment economy — coordinating in-office days so that presence is intentional, not coincidental. A new generation of tools makes this easy.

Platforms like Café let colleagues align schedules, connect with internal communities, and surface real-life events, while Scoop shows who's coming in and when, making it simple to plan around the people who actually matter to your work.

Give Them Reasons to Come to the Office: If you want people to leave the comfort of their homes, you need to give them a reason worth the commute — not a mandate, but a genuine pull.

Microsoft's Work Trend Index found that 84% of employees say they need more than a vague sense of obligation to make the effort. What they actually crave is human connection and collaboration that can only happen in person.

Accenture calls this "Earning the Commute" — the idea that in-office time should be purposeful enough that people genuinely want to show up. The goal isn't butts in seats. It's creating experiences compelling enough to make people say: yeah, I'd commute for that.

Make the Office a High-Profile Destination: For most people, the office is a place they tolerate — not one they look forward to. But what if it were a destination? Somewhere compelling enough to compete with the comfort of home?

The organizations getting this right are treating the office less like a workspace and more like a curated experience — bringing in customers to share how employees' work has impacted them, hosting inspiring speakers, creating opportunities for meaningful exposure to leaders.

One client built a full calendar of experiential events — speakers, concerts, volunteer days, escape rooms — and saw attendance climb steadily as the office became somewhere people actually wanted to be. Connection and meaning don't happen by mandate. They happen by design.

Access to Leaders and High Performers: The office is also the natural home for development experiences that don't translate well to a screen. One client created a shadowing program pairing employees with senior leaders for full days — observing real decisions, asking questions, and learning the kind of institutional wisdom that rarely makes it into a formal training.

Role-play workshops for high-stakes skills like negotiating, public speaking, or delivering difficult feedback are equally well-suited to in-person settings, where the energy of the room is part of the learning.

Listen, Experiment, and Iterate: According to data from the Future Forum, most post-pandemic planning happens without any direct input from employees, which could worsen things.

A lack of flexibility is one of the top reasons why people continue to quit their jobs. Workers who don't have the flexibility to manage their schedules are three times more likely to look for new opportunities. This trend is also reflected in the job market, with fully remote job postings receiving 50% of all job applications on LinkedIn.

Listen to your people and what they need to be most effective. No one has all the answers. We've never done this before. We all need to be empathetic and curious.

Performance Management for Corporate Athletes

According to Gallup, only 14% of employees feel their performance reviews inspire them to improve, and they are so bad that they make performance worse in about a third of cases.

Since its inception, the annual performance review has been a broken way to assess performance. If you think about elite performers in any realm, they get constant real-time feedback and coaching, which they integrate and then use to pivot quickly.

Why would organizations stockpile feedback for an entire year just to throw it all up on people at the annual review? At this point, the feedback is out of context and difficult to act on, which causes resentment and erodes trust. This helps no one.

Performance management must transform into a real-time, ongoing conversation focused on goals, development, and measurement. Our Gen Z and Millennial colleagues are used to getting constant feedback from parents, peers, and the environment, so they expect it at work.

However, we need to acknowledge that not everyone is comfortable giving and receiving feedback. Feedback can cause what Dr. David Rock of the NeuroLeadership Institute calls a "threat response"—the fight-or-flight feeling that occurs when an imminent physical threat exists in a person's environment. They've shown that when people even hear the word "feedback," a part of the brain lights up indicating threat, and when people feel threatened, their brain basically shuts down.

Microsoft brought Dr. Rock in to revamp its feedback system. During the process, they found a way around the knee-jerk reaction to feedback. They found that having people proactively ask for feedback reduced the threat response and cognitive stress by 30%.

This became the foundation of their Perspectives program, which encourages employees to solicit opinions from their peers in a structured way. Enabling employees to offer their perspective on their own performance first reduces status threats. The program deliberately does not refer to the information as "feedback," and the prompts feel more like coaching conversations than reviews.

Asking someone for feedback in this way has significant positive psychological effects, like getting another person's buy-in. When we ask managers and co-workers for feedback this way, it makes them feel trusted and more invested in our success.

As Dr. Robert Cialdini (the godfather of persuasion) has found in study after study, giving advice "puts a person in a merging state of mind, which stimulates the linking of one's identity with another party's." This makes them feel more connected and more invested in the person asking.

Cialdini's research shows three things happen when someone feels they have been involved in another person's career this way: they rate the result more highly, they see themselves as being more responsible for the result, and they think more highly of the people who asked them for advice.

The takeaway: Organizations can harness the benefits of feedback without the pitfalls by building a culture that normalizes people proactively asking managers and colleagues for feedback. This helps build relationships, improve performance, and build the muscle of self-awareness.

Choose-Your-Own-Adventure Career Pathing

One-size-fits-all career ladders must be reimagined into omni-dimensional lattices that leverage different individuals' strengths, preferences, and life seasons. Today's workforce is not content with traditional, linear career trajectories.

Instead, they crave growth in their earning power and achievements. They yearn for the freedom to live on their terms, unrestrained by geographical boundaries, and empowered by the value they create through their intellectual capital. For them, success is not measured by the hours they work but by the impact they make.

Millennials and Gen Zs live their life on a different time horizon than previous generations and don't share the "I'll be a slave until I retire" mindset. Because they've grown up in a different world, their approach is a more sustainable integration of hustle and flow throughout their day, career, and life. They want expanded career pathways with increased choice, flexibility, and personalization in how they grow and experience their career.

And this doesn't just mean linear advancement. McKinsey found offering lateral career opportunities is two-and-a-half times more predictive of employee retention than compensation and twelve times more predictive than promotions. It also shows that 60% of workers changed companies to advance because their companies didn't have those opportunities.

It's critical to have robust career paths that include linear and lateral moves for people of all levels of the organization.

Regardless of what your pathways look like, it's key—especially for your younger workforce—that the organization makes it clear how they get from one role to another. Provide testimonials with a day-in-the-life view, so people can see exactly what skills and experiences they need, how to get to the next level, and what success looks like with clear KPIs, expectations, and estimated timing.

I would approach this like a video game, so they can see the path ahead, their progress toward it, and celebrate when they achieve milestones. In the future, careers will increasingly be designed according to an employee's interests and skills. AI-based software offerings such as Gloat, Fuel50, and Flux are the leaders in a growing pack of platforms that build career paths in this way.

Unfortunately, the antiquated model of progression used in most organizations today tends to produce ill-equipped and, perhaps, even ill-intentioned managers, with downstream effects of stifled and disengaged employees.

This limited model dictates that if people want to progress or get paid more, they need to manage others. So, organizations reward the stellar individual contributor with the title of manager and more responsibility. This often comes without additional training or support, only to actualize the Peter Principle of promoting people to their level of incompetence. The skills of a rockstar individual contributor are often the opposite of those of a good manager. Employees are being set up to fail without additional training, coaching, and support.

We'll dive into how organizations can better support managers in Chapter 8. Still, from a purely structural perspective, one way to tackle this issue is to bifurcate career progression tracks the way 3M and Mastercard have. They have dual career tracks to the top—one for individual contributors who want to continue sharpening their subject-matter expertise, and another for people who want to manage and develop others.

PwC has been a longstanding leader in investing in its employees. Recently, the firm doubled down on its people experience and value proposition by investing $2.4 billion over the next few years in a new program called My+. My+ provides increased choice, flexibility, personalization, and a focus on holistic well-being.

The program provides elevated leadership development, comprehensive and à la carte benefits options, and the ability for their people to choose the number of hours they want to work and the types of assignments they take on.

The program makes it acceptable to be honest about how people like to work. For example, if Susan is in a more ambitious season of life and wants to work sixty to eighty hours a week, Jake is seventy years old and looking to return to the workforce part-time, and Trey has a side hustle they want to nurture—all of those paths look different. All of these situations can be accommodated as long as there is transparency and clear expectations are set.

Another often-overlooked option organizations can offer people at all points in their career journey is role sharing. While the idea isn't new, few organizations leverage it. Roleshare is one of several new platforms designed to help companies attract untapped talent and mobilize employees who want flexibility by matching them to share full-time jobs with other employees.

We've also seen a rise in fractional roles that are divided among more than one person as a way to access top talent. These enable scaling up quickly without making lengthy commitments while providing increased flexibility to employees. Some organizations leverage this by bringing in retired employees for a few months to backfill a colleague on maternity leave or while searching for a new full-time person for the role.

We are also starting to see the transition from job-based careers toward skills-based roles and projects. The skills-based model has many upsides, including increased diversity, inclusivity, and expansion of the talent pool. It also increases the agility and relevance of the organization's capabilities. For example, perhaps a stay-at-home mom without a college degree can come into the workforce as a rockstar project manager now that her kids are grown. Or a former Uber driver who taught himself to code can now join a finance organization as an IT expert.

Internal career marketplaces (which we'll look at in Chapter 12) are another great way to explore this in your organization.

Aiming to become more relevant in the evolving world of work requires more than just updating outdated workplace practices and ways of working. While this is a great starting point, it is essential to intentionally redesign your culture to effectively implement the new ways of working and align them with your strategy.

Chapter 5

Is Your Culture Driving Strategy or Burning It Down?

The saying "culture eats strategy for breakfast" is a vast understatement.

Culture will make or break your organization in the form of profitability, productivity, engagement, agility, collaboration, innovation, customer satisfaction, burnout, turnover, and healthcare costs.

Culture is happening all the time, so you need to be deliberate and leverage it strategically. A major MIT study found toxic cultures to be the largest predictor of the Great Resignation. This came up ten times more than the runners-up—compensation and work-life balance.

Toxic culture is cancerous and includes exclusion, disrespect, lack of recognition, politics, bullying, discrimination, harassment, and cutthroat behavior.

Besides the $223 billion cost of attrition due to toxic cultures, the cost of lower performance of those who stay in the organization is another $2,000 billion. The business case for cultivating a great culture is compelling.

When aligned, consistent, and leveraged appropriately, culture is the highest-impact and the most inexpensive lever you can pull to deliver the business strategy and create the X-factor that engages and retains talent.

Culture stealthily clarifies expectations, what's important, and how things get done. When everyone is operating from these values, it bonds all the unique people in the organization and shows them how to be successful.

It also provides continuity in the face of change, disruption, and the inevitability of coming and going employees.

But I don't have to tell you this. New research from MIT shows 90% of leaders know the importance of culture and its impact on the organization's performance. Still, only 15% are doing anything about it because they think it's too complicated or time-consuming.

As someone who has helped organizations of all sizes and industries evolve and transform their culture, I can tell you it's not complicated. Still, it does require leaders to be deliberate and vigilant.

So let's take a look at how to defines culture.

What Culture Is

Many people mistakenly believe culture is simply free lunch or the words on a wall in the office. However, culture runs much deeper than that. It can be sensed in every interaction.

Culture is like the lifestyle of the organization—it governs how people interact, how things get done, and what behaviors are tolerated. It transcends physical space. For example, whether people are at a client site, at a work happy hour, sending an email during their commute, or working from home, they demonstrate the culture in how they interact.

Culture operationalizes the true values of the organization, the values people live daily, which are not necessarily the ones on the wall. This is why leaders need to be very intentional to ensure the values they live and allow to exist are the ones they want to permeate the organization.

Culture is a daily practice. It's constantly evolving as the business and people do. If you see something off-culture and do nothing, you've created a new culture. If you think of culture as the air the organization breathes, everyone is responsible for ensuring it is healthy, life-giving, and consistently lived.

The best way to quantify your culture is whether you're achieving your business goals. If you're not, it's likely a culture problem.

Culture should be designed and leveraged to drive the organization's business strategy by reverse engineering it based on the organization's goals, mission, and purpose.

You then build your culture to deliver it through the environment, behaviors, and experiences. For example, if an organization needs to be more innovative, a culture of curiosity, growth mindset, psychological safety, risk-taking, and experimenting is necessary.

This means leaders must show vulnerability and role-model risk-taking. They also need to tell stories of others taking risks, highlighting how it contributes directly to the organization's goal of becoming more innovative. These behaviors should also be built into performance evaluations, KPIs, and other systems to reinforce them.

What Effective Culture Looks Like

There is no one-size-fits-all culture that works for every organization. But, if I were to describe a healthy culture that enables the people and the business to thrive, it would prioritize learning, curiosity, respect, inclusion, and recognition.

- Curiosity plays a crucial role in fostering openness and acceptance of ideas.

- A growth mindset is essential for experimentation, embracing "failure," and continuously iterating.

- Respect and inclusion create an environment where people can bring their differences and unique creativity to the work.

- Recognition and appreciation is the most effective reinforcement for innovative risk-taking and producing great work.

Regardless of the type of culture leaders want to engender, alignment between what they say they stand for and how they behave is critical for the culture to be effective. The first sign of a leader not walking the talk, or shying away from punishing off-culture behavior, and they lose all credibility.

The sign of a strong culture is people holding each other accountable for behaving in alignment with the values. Marc Benioff saw this when two of his female employees brought to his attention that Salesforce was paying their male and female employees unequally. Equality is one of their four core values. While he had been surprised to hear it, he immediately ordered an audit of all Salesforce employee salaries.

To address the root cause of the issue, the team devised a new set of job codes and standards and applied them across the organization to ensure everyone performing similar work was similarly compensated from day one.

From there, the team began reviewing merit increases, bonuses, stock grants, and promotions to root out disparities. As of today, Salesforce has spent over $10.3 million addressing the differences in pay based on gender, race, and ethnicity.

It's worth noting that the strongest cultural signals are almost never the big, formal ones—the all-hands speeches, the values posters, the annual culture survey. They are the small, daily, unremarkable moments: how a leader responds when someone brings them bad news; whether a manager defends a junior employee who was talked over in a meeting; whether the person who cuts corners gets promoted or called out.

Culture lives in these micro-moments. It is made and unmade in them continuously. Leaders who understand this watch those moments carefully—and act in them deliberately.

Great cultures, like the one that has evolved at Microsoft since Satya Nadella took over, continue to attract, cultivate, and retain high performers.

Several years ago, Microsoft was a very different place. While they were financially fine, Nadella saw cracks beneath the surface when he took over. He decided they would undertake a major cultural transformation.

Over nine months, they went from being a culture of "know-it-alls" to one of "learn-it-alls" with a growth mindset. Today Microsoft is the most valuable company in the world.

So how did they do it? The inspiration came from Carol Dweck's work around a growth mindset. Her work highlights differences between people who hold a fixed mindset (one that says intelligence and ability are static) and those with a growth mindset (which believes these qualities can be learned and developed).

Today, Microsoft's culture encourages people to constantly develop themselves, learn new things, and operate from a place of curiosity. This culture shift has led to 89% of employees saying they are proud to work there, and 93% of employees would recommend Microsoft as a great workplace.

Guiding principles of cultivating a learning culture like the one at Microsoft include:

Leaders Show Vulnerability and Humility: This inspires teams to learn from mistakes and pursue continuous growth. Demonstrating that they don't have all the answers and embracing failure as a learning opportunity creates a culture where experimentation and risk-taking are encouraged.

Create a Safe-To-Fail Environment: Sharing learnings and encouraging low-stakes experimentation fosters a culture where everyone feels empowered to take risks and try new things.

Managers Become Coaches: Providing guidance, support, and constructive criticism creates an environment where everyone is encouraged to learn and improve.

Omnidirectional Feedback: Encouraging feedback from all levels of the organization opens up communication channels and creates a culture of transparency, trust, and accountability.

Meaningful Metrics: You create a culture of accountability and continuous improvement by measuring how you develop others and grow yourself. Whether through performance evaluations, personal development plans, or other tools, metrics can help you track progress and identify areas for growth.

How Culture Trips Organizations Up

There is often a misconception that leaders "create a culture" by dropping some nice words into a PowerPoint deck or slapping them on the wall, and expecting everyone to behave in alignment.

Instead, leaders need to create the conditions for the behaviors they want to see, and the result is the culture.

This happens when leaders role-model the behaviors aligned with the values, spotlight examples of others demonstrating them, and hold people accountable for doing the same.

One of the reasons it's critical to protect against a toxic culture lies in the phenomenon known as the "contagion effect." This concept is exemplified by the renowned Jim Rohn quote: "You become the average of the five people you spend the most time with."

The contagion effect is happening all the time beneath the surface through the spread of behaviors, attitudes, and emotions from person to person. Have you ever been in a meeting with a "Debbie Downer" who sucks the energy out of the room?

Or, on the flip side, have you ever left an interaction with someone who's positive, energetic, and inspiring, and you find yourself feeling motivated and ready to take on the world?

These are examples of emotional contagion at play. As social animals, our mirror neurons in the cerebral cortex tend to mimic those we come in contact with—in person or even on a video call. The saying "neurons that fire together, wire together" is relevant here.

The pathways in our brains that mimic others' moods and behaviors become stronger the more they are activated. Thus, it's paramount to prioritize safeguarding against what you don't want your culture to be.

Addressing toxic culture isn't just a nice-to-have—it's a matter of strategically protecting the organization from the powerful and subtle ways a few bad actors negatively impact the environment.

Research by Will Felps at the University of Sydney has uncovered some shocking truths about how even one "bad apple" can have a ripple effect on others. Felps found that when a low performer or toxic person is present, other team members start adopting those same behaviors, causing their performance to drop by an average of 40%.

To guard against this situation, companies like Netflix have taken a bold approach by creating a talent-dense environment that promotes high performance. Based on research that found top engineers to be ten times more effective than average engineers, Netflix's rock star principle has become the cornerstone of its talent strategy.

By only hiring and retaining employees who operate at a rock star level and paying them more, Netflix has created a culture of excellence where people hold themselves and each other to a high standard.

Toxic Culture Root Causes and Solutions

Incongruence

The impact can be devastating when an organization's actions don't align with its stated values. Leaders who fail to live up to their standards or turn a blind eye to off-culture behavior send a dangerous message: it's okay to say one thing and do another. This duplicity erodes trust and undermines the foundations of a healthy workplace culture.

To avoid this kind of incongruence, leaders must consistently and authentically model the behaviors they expect from others. They need to hold themselves accountable and be willing to call out others when they fall short.

When leaders lead by example and hold others to the same standard, they create a culture of integrity, respect, and trust that will help their organization thrive.

Leaders Not Leading

Like an absent parent in the family system, when leaders fail to set the vision and structures that guide, inspire, and hold people accountable, it creates silos, politics, and an environment of uncertainty, anxiety, and chaos. This means no one is focusing on the actual work.

Build a culture of alignment by increasing transparency. Ensure everyone understands the company's vision, purpose, and mission and how their work fits the bigger picture. This includes establishing clear roles and shared goals for each team so they can see the impact of their work.

Shared purpose is often the most powerful antidote to silos. Use it as a starting point — and build from there by encouraging team leaders to open their meetings to other departments, giving colleagues a window into work they'd otherwise never see.

Remove barriers to collaboration by investing in tools and data sources that communicate with each other. Establish cross-mentoring programs to encourage knowledge transfer and learning between teams.

Fostering transparency, breaking down silos, and aligning incentives will help you build a collaborative culture that drives success for the entire organization.

Consider rewarding teams rather than individual top performers to promote a sense of shared success. Microsoft even added questions to performance reviews that highlight how each employee's work impacts and benefits others.

A Lack of Transparency, Especially At Critical Times

In today's world, where everyone is a broadcaster, if your organization doesn't provide people with information and updates as quickly as possible, they'll see it on social media, eroding trust faster than you can send a tweet.

When there is a lack of transparency across the organization about how things work, how the business is doing, or the impacts of upcoming changes, it creates distrust and increases anxiety.

In a dearth of information, our brains start creating stories to make sense of things—and these stories are rarely good.

It's paramount for leaders to communicate early and often, especially during times of change and uncertainty. Even if they don't have all the answers, all they need to say is that they don't know, are working on it, and will come back with the answer.

This level of transparency and vulnerability builds trust and quells the rumors that will otherwise spread across the organization.

Tolerating Bad Actors

We've all heard of the "no asshole rule," but unfortunately, it's all too common for organizations to turn a blind eye to such behavior.

It may be the rainmaker sales bro who treats everyone terribly but gets to stick around because he brings in so much revenue. Sometimes it's the micromanager or gaslighting bully who has secured her spot because she is great at kissing up and kicking down.

Tolerating bad behavior is like a disease that spreads and infects everything around it. Research shows that such behavior can reduce the performance of those around them by up to 40%—and that's not even considering the mental health, productivity loss, burnout, and attrition these bad actors cause.

Organizations must take proactive steps to address this issue. Leaders can start by asking employees about their experiences and where there are hurdles to doing their best work. They should also provide channels for anonymous feedback, implement regular 360-degree reviews, and audit exit interviews.

Having a culture of psychological safety is key so that individuals can speak candidly without fear of retaliation.

It's also essential for leaders to share stories of bad behavior candidly in town halls or other communication channels and discuss the actions taken to address it. This demonstrates zero tolerance for such behavior.

A Lack Of Candor

At the other end of the spectrum, organizations can see a culture of mediocrity and passive aggression because people want to be "nice" and, as a result, don't hold each other accountable.

One way to counter this is to create a culture of real-time feedback. Because most people are not naturally comfortable or skilled at giving effective feedback, it's critical to ensure everyone at all levels is trained, comfortable, and committed to giving and receiving ongoing feedback.

Kim Scott has a great model for implementing what she calls Radical Candor, which provides an easy way to show candor with care. As she says, it's key to care personally and challenge others directly. The highest-performing teams leverage feedback and ensure open conversations are constantly flowing, up, down, and laterally.

An easy way to scale this is the After Action Review (AAR) model, first used by the military. At the end of every meeting, save a few minutes to address three questions: What went well? What didn't go well? What will we do differently next time? It's simple, and because people expect it as part of the meeting cadence, there's no feeling of being emotionally hijacked or taking it personally.

A Lack Of Psychological Safety

In a culture dominated by fear, people are hesitant to express themselves, hindering creativity and risk-taking. So much time is spent covering one's butt that the work becomes secondary.

Psychological safety is a precursor to engagement, innovation, and high performance. It encourages open communication, experimentation, and accountability without fear of judgment or punishment.

Environments lacking psychological safety lead to information hoarding, silos, bureaucracy, and blame. Like trust, psychological safety acts as an organizational lubricant. When present, it reduces internal threats and allows teams to focus on seizing opportunities and protecting the organization from external dangers.

There are many ways to create psychological safety:

- Leaders set the tone by openly admitting mistakes and sharing moments of vulnerability.

- Call out pink elephants and name the silent problems—ask people to list all the issues that are being avoided, and remind them that as a team, you can only solve the problems that are made explicit.

- Instead of singling out the person causing issues, turn the issue into a collective problem to solve.

- Celebrate the messenger—when someone steps forward with bad news or a "failure," show appreciation and respect for taking the risk and focus on what the team can learn from it. Normalize what TED speaker Matt Smith calls taking a "failure bow," where a person can say, "Oops, I forgot to do X—I need to take a failure bow."

Lego has unlocked a way to create a psychologically safe workplace through the power of play. They created an environment where tough conversations and decision-making are encouraged and welcomed. With playful symbols and practices such as office campfires made out of Lego bricks, employees come together to focus on the matter at hand, free from fear of retribution. This innovative approach has led to employee engagement soaring.

Inequality

Consider working in an organization where the playing field is not level, where leaders show favoritism, certain privileges are reserved for the elite, and promotions are based on who puts in the most face time. It's a breeding ground for mistrust and counterproductive politicking.

Without equity and fairness, productivity, engagement, and morale will suffer.

To counteract this toxic environment, transparency is critical. The more transparency around expectations, processes, and decision-making, the less room there is for unfairness to hide. But it's not just about fairness—it's also about inclusion.

When employees feel excluded or experience microaggressions and have to engage in code-switching, they're closer to burnout than anyone else. These emotional stressors drain cognitive resources, increase anxiety, and erode psychological safety. You're not getting the best out of your talent when they feel they can't be themselves at work. Inclusion—which we'll get into in detail in Chapter 7—isn't just a trendy buzzword; it's crucial for creating a thriving workplace.

Research shows that when people feel excluded, it registers in the brain as if they're experiencing physical pain. The implications for health and well-being are significant. An inclusive culture is over three times more likely to inspire employees to deliver their best work.

Hustle Culture

We've all heard the siren song of hustle culture: "Work harder, work longer, and never stop grinding." But let's be real—after a certain point, the law of diminishing returns kicks in. Stanford researchers found that productivity per hour drops off a cliff after fifty hours a week, and after fifty-five hours, you might as well be banging your head against the wall.

Apparently, Elon Musk didn't get that memo. He recently laid the law to his Twitter "minions," demanding they show they are "hardcore" and work "long hours at a high intensity" or face the consequences. Not surprisingly, this ultimatum didn't go over well, and many employees chose to opt out instead of burning out.

Listen, I get it—as a self-proclaimed, proud workaholic, sometimes you need to grind to get things done. However, if your culture is all grind, all the time, it will breed nothing but stress, resentment, and burnout. We'll share ways to mitigate this in Chapter 9.

How to Audit, Evolve, and Operationalize Culture

In the most successful cultures, you see leadership models it, HR scales it, managers drive it, and everyone lives it.

A great place to start is to reverse engineer your mission and strategy and determine the values and behaviors that will enable their success. These daily practices become your culture, and if consistently implemented, will help you deliver on your mission and goals.

But how do you ensure that everyone in your organization embodies these values? Leaders need to role-model them every day and hold others accountable. Embed the values into processes and systems, and create rituals that ground them in daily moments. Continuously talk about the values, why culture matters, and the importance of everyone living them. Train employees on how to embody them in their daily behaviors and help them see how doing so contributes to the mission and purpose of the organization.

It's key to co-create the culture with employees, asking them to submit videos, quotes, and other materials that exemplify what the culture means to them. You can leverage these in your communications, social media, and promotional videos.

Don't forget to measure how well your people are embodying your culture and develop performance metrics that reward behaviors that align with your values. Mastercard, for example, ties job performance to how well employees demonstrate their newly established culture. This makes the desired behaviors sticky and provides accountability.

While culture, when done right, can drive the organizational strategy by steering daily behaviors, people also need to know where they are going and why. That is where purpose comes in.

Chapter 6

Give Them Something To Believe In

Today's workforce and consumers are more intentional and discerning about the companies they choose to associate with. Shared values are key, and authenticity is a must.

The new generation isn't content with just any job or product; they are on the hunt for an inspiring ethos and a shared commitment to making a positive impact on the world. They need to know that the organizations they work for and buy from are driven by a purpose that extends beyond mere profit.

These expectations require companies to operate very differently; taking responsibility for their actions and consider their social impact.

The latest generation of workers doesn't just want a paycheck—they crave purpose and fulfillment from their work. They want to be a part of an organization that is truly making a difference in the world, one that is committed to meaningful change.

Purpose is a powerful way to signal shared values in today's crowded marketplace and talent pool.

While selling socks and T-shirts may not sound particularly aspirational, Bombas, for example, has shown that it can be a powerful tool for change. What sets Bombas apart is their authentic commitment to their purpose. They align their actions with their values and principles, creating a meaningful impact on the world.

When they first started, they recognized that socks were the most requested item in homeless shelters, and they knew they had to take action. They set out to create the most comfortable and durable socks that would provide a sense of dignity and comfort to those in need.

For every item purchased, they generously donate the same item to those experiencing homelessness—a contribution that has now reached over 50 million items.

Purpose is a high-value, no-cost lever to balance the interests of all stakeholders while keeping an eye on the bottom line.

The Value of Purpose

A recent Deloitte study found that purpose-oriented companies have higher productivity, three times higher growth rates, a more satisfied workforce, 30% higher levels of innovation, and 40% higher levels of retention than their competitors.

McKinsey research shows 89% of employees believe it's important for their company to have a purpose, and 70% say they are likely to recommend that company to others if inspired by its purpose.

This is valuable to customers as well. Research shows 25% of consumers are willing to pay more if a brand raises its prices to be more environmentally and socially responsible or to pay higher wages to its employees.

When it comes to the market, we've seen 10x the return for what co-founder of Conscious Capitalism, Raj Sisodia, calls "Firms of Endearment." These organizations who take action for people and the planet—grew 14% faster than other businesses last year and in the past 17 years, grew by 1,681% compared to the S&P 500 average of 118%.

The hard value of purpose is clear, but let's look at why it creates results.

The Purpose of Purpose

Purpose is a strategic tool to guide the organization, build trust, garner respect, and inspire motivation, pride, and commitment. Don't mistake the purpose for clever tweets, catchy ads, or a marketing campaign. Those things have their place, but the organizational purpose is much more strategic and should drive business decisions.

A key function of purpose, when lived authentically, is to serve as an orientation point so that the organization can find its way when changes, disruption, and difficult decisions come—and they will. When you're clear on the organization's purpose, it's easier to stay on track, know what is important to pursue, and attract the right people to help deliver it.

Purpose can inform what choices make sense in both the short and long term. CVS, for example, proved its purpose was its guiding light when it removed tobacco from its shelves because it didn't align with its evolved purpose to "Bring Their Heart to Everyone's Health." While it took a loss of $2 billion initially, it has since increased the share price by 30% month after month.

Purpose Guides Leaders On Which Issues to Speak On

Today's employees and customers expect your organization's purpose to be clear and lived authentically. The purpose should guide everything leaders and the organization do, even at the expense of profits.

The Edelman Trust Barometer shows that as trust in government and the media continues to spiral, people have an even greater expectation of business to lead in the world. 81% of employees want their organization to give them a voice by speaking out on issues they care about. We experienced this viscerally during the 2020 social justice movement after the murder of George Floyd.

Leaders and organizations can no longer hang out on the sidelines. They need to have a clear sense of what they stand for, an authentic point of view, and the willingness to amplify the voices of their people.

Salesforce CEO Marc Benioff did this in 2015 when then-governor Mike Pence signed the Religious Freedom Restoration Act (RFRA) in Indiana. Many proponents believed it targeted LGBT people and other groups. Marc spoke out against the law, threatening to scale back Salesforce's investment in the state, followed by announcing plans to remove Salesforce's presence in Indiana.

Ultimately, he offered Salesforce employees residing in Indiana relocation packages to transfer elsewhere. After a week of other CEOs rallying to fight the law as well, Pence approved a revised version of it, explicitly banning businesses from refusing service because of a person's sexual orientation or gender identity.

If you want employees and customers to truly believe in you, you need to be willing to take a stand for the organization's purpose—even when it's hard.

Purpose Builds Trust By Setting Expectations

Operating from purpose builds trust by exhibiting what the organization stands for and how its decisions are guided. However, just like with values and culture, alignment is crucial to its effectiveness.

Purpose washing is not a good look. When a company announces its purpose but the pithy words in the ad campaign don't govern the behavior of senior leadership or how the organization operates, everyone recognizes the hypocrisy and becomes cynical.

In our hyper-transparent world, people are made aware in real time when an organization's leaders or practices are not authentically aligned with what it says its purpose is.

Nike learned this the hard way. After they launched campaigns around female empowerment several years ago, they were sued by ex-employees for gender discrimination, bias, inequitable pay, and sexual harassment.

Despite Nike's 2018 "Dream Crazy" campaign with Colin Kaepernick, under 9% of Nike's directors were Black at that time. The purpose must be more than just a marketing campaign or a bolt-on program. It must drive the business and people strategies.

Nike has since put their money where their mouth is in addressing systemic racism. In 2020, they committed $140 million to invest in and support organizations focused on economic empowerment, education, and social justice. As they work to address racial inequality, their website transparently tracks where they are on the journey.

Purpose Aligns and Unites Stakeholders

A clear and compelling purpose can be a powerful tool in bringing an organization's stakeholders together. Purpose serves as a common goal that aligns the efforts of everyone involved, providing direction, meaning, and motivation.

When stakeholders share a sense of purpose, it can overcome individual agendas and siloed thinking, fostering a sense of unity and cooperation toward a shared objective. This is the essence of stakeholder capitalism, where the interests of all parties are considered and integrated.

Purpose Gives People Something to Believe In

An effective organizational purpose is more than just a mission statement—it's a rallying cry for greatness in service of a greater good. It's a reminder that the collective efforts of the people connected to the organization can make a meaningful impact on the world, just by being a part of it.

When an organization's purpose integrates both business and societal interests, it motivates employees and makes them proud to be a part of something bigger than themselves. Better yet, when people have a clear understanding of their role in achieving the organization's purpose, they feel like they're part of something truly special.

How to Determine the Organizational Purpose

Purpose has to resonate with people's hearts and minds if it is going to motivate them. The average employee is not inspired by being part of "the most customer-centric company on the planet" (Amazon) or "to be the best financial services company in the world" (JPMorgan).

Statements like these fall flat and don't evoke a desire to invest one's time, energy, and discretionary effort into the company. So organizations need to be thoughtful about what they are trying to accomplish in the world beyond profit, and why. Leaders must ensure the purpose is conveyed across the organization in a way that resonates with people.

A good example of this is what Hubert Joly did several years ago as CEO of Best Buy. As he puts it, "If I had joined the company and said, 'The key thing we're going to do in the next few years is double the share price or the earnings per share,' who would've cared? This is not motivating. And so what we did was redefine who we were."

With a bold vision in mind, Joly proclaimed, "We are not just a consumer electronics retailer. We are a company that's in the business of enriching lives through technology by addressing key human needs." This transformative shift not only inspired the entire organization, but also expanded the company's market potential exponentially.

Discovering a Purpose

A few years ago, I stepped into a new leadership role in a customer experience company looking to increase employee engagement, collaboration, and retention. I started by partnering with leaders across the organization to embark on a journey to uncover its true purpose.

I began with a deep listening tour that revealed a common theme—the workforce yearned to make a positive impact on their communities and society at large. They spent the majority of their time on the phone with customers, trying to solve problems.

We worked with a cross-sample of employees to make it a reality by connecting this desire to make a positive impact to their day-to-day role in call centers across the globe. The result was an authentic and resonant purpose: "Changing the world one conversation at a time."

The workforce was enthusiastically committed to it because they helped shape it and were able to see how to live it in their daily calls with customers, in team discussions, and in monthly community events.

By tapping into the deepest needs of the employees and including them in articulating the purpose, we ignited a passion that permeated throughout the organization and produced an uptick in our retention and engagement scores.

Crafting a Purpose

Crafting a compelling purpose for your organization can be challenging, but tactics used in social movements can be powerful in connecting with your audience.

The key is to identify a problem or dissatisfaction in the world that your company or industry can help solve. By doing so, you can articulate what your organization stands for in the fight for a better future.

Take one of my clients in the healthcare space. They have a front-row seat to seeing how our society is becoming less and less healthy, and paying more for healthcare than any other Western industrialized nation. This dissatisfaction led them to create a purpose that would empower people to take a more active role in their well-being.

Their purpose provided a platform for rousing patients and caregivers toward a common goal of partnership in healthcare. As a result, they were able to raise employee engagement from 39% to 29% and improve readmission rates and length-of-stay metrics.

Designing a Purpose

If you are looking for a more structured approach to ensure that your corporate purpose is a true driving force behind your business strategy, here is a framework to use.

The first step is to identify the key internal constituencies that have a stake in your purpose, from demand generation to HR to strategy, governance, sustainability, and employees.

Establishing a working team with representatives from each of these groups can ensure that your purpose is truly comprehensive and inclusive.

Next, you need to find an idea that transcends the vested interests of each stakeholder:

- **Does your business model create value for society** in unusual ways for your industry? If so, you may want to have a purpose like Bombas socks or Warby Parker, who both offer "you buy one, we donate one" business models.

- **Do you deliver value to customers** while also being an attractive employer? If so, you may want to land on a culture-based purpose like WD-40 Company, which focuses on creating positive lasting memories. They do this by cultivating a tribal culture of learning and teaching, which produces a highly engaged workforce who live their company's values every day. WD-40 may not sound particularly sexy—they make a multipurpose lubricant in a can. However, 93% of employees report being engaged, 91% are proud to work there, and they've had 13% annual returns for the past twenty-five years.

- **Does your organization have a history** of standing for something in the market? Purpose is most powerful when it's credible — earned through consistent action rather than declared from a podium. Patagonia's assertion that it is "in business to save our home planet" lands because Yvon Chouinard has spent decades proving it.

Grounding your purpose design in a co-creative process and gathering input from a wide range of stakeholders will help ensure that your purpose statement is authentic, relevant, and strategic.

Remember: the purpose must be more than just a marketing campaign or a bolt-on program. It must drive the business and people strategies, from how you hire and develop people, to how you make decisions, to the causes you speak out on.

When it does all of that, it becomes one of the most powerful forces in your organization.

Activating the Purpose

Having a purpose is great, but if you don't activate it, you're wasting everyone's time.

If your company's purpose is just a sentence in the annual CEO letter, or if you talk about being purpose-driven without following through, you will not realize the benefits outlined at the beginning of this chapter.

A recent study found 80% of executives know the value of purpose, but only 40% feel their purpose is well articulated and understood by their people.

Purpose needs to be activated internally and externally to bring it to life and ensure flow through the entire organization.

Harvard Business Review found leadership teams who activate their purpose see a 2,530% increase in productivity and retention.

Purpose Is a Team Sport

Purpose can't be owned by marketing any more than culture can be owned by HR. Purpose needs to be led by leaders and owned by everyone. Senior leaders must actively relate to organizational purpose, allowing purpose to guide their decision-making and their leadership style.

Leaders can't treat it as an initiative or program; it's not finite. It needs to be an ongoing drumbeat woven into everything. Leaders must bring purpose to life through constant, authentic communication and storytelling.

It's key to hold activation sessions with the top leaders to socialize the details around the why, what, who, how, etc., and provide them with talking points, expectations, and ways they can live it.

If the purpose remains just a poster on a wall, it will not impact and motivate employees. Only by actively embodying and communicating the organizational purpose can leaders inspire their people. Leaders can share visceral examples and stories that bring the purpose to life.

One of my clients, the CEO of a renewable energy company, shares a powerful story about visiting a remote village that had no access to electricity, describing the transformative impact of installing solar panels in the community.

Through vivid details, he paints the picture of children who were now able to study at night, families having access to clean water, and local businesses thriving—all thanks to the company's commitment to sustainable energy solutions.

The Purpose Is the Red Thread

Once leaders begin bringing purpose to life, the next challenge is embedding it everywhere. That means identifying the behaviors that bring your purpose to life, ensuring every employee understands how to model them, and reflecting that purpose across every touchpoint — job descriptions, performance reviews, internal communications, and symbols.

The most committed organizations don't just talk about purpose — they measure it. Internal scorecards, engagement surveys, and business metrics can all track awareness and connection to purpose over time. Procter & Gamble goes further, tying executive compensation directly to purpose metrics — a clear signal that emotional leverage and financial results are linked.

KPMG offers one of the most compelling examples of purpose activation at scale. Employees were invited to answer a simple question — "What do you do at KPMG?" — with a purpose-driven headline. "I Combat Terrorism." "I Restore Eyesight." Each response became a poster featuring the employee's photo and the firm's collective purpose: "Inspire Confidence and Empower Change." To gamify it, leaders promised two extra holiday days if staff could create 10,000 posters by Thanksgiving.

They received 42,000.

Engagement scores hit record highs. Pride in work surged. KPMG climbed thirty-one places on Fortune's 100 Best Companies to Work For list — reaching number twelve and becoming the highest-ranked of the Big Four. Recruiting improved. Turnover dropped.

Chapter 7

The Cheat Code for Engagement

Why would anyone join, stay, or give you their best if your organization fails to create an environment where they feel safe, included, and welcome?

This is also important to your customers, who increasingly want to see themselves represented by the people in your organization.

Diversity, equity, inclusion, and belonging (DEIB) are the precursor to attracting, engaging, and unlocking high performance in your people, as well as innovation and customer experience.

Diversity, Equity, Inclusion, and Belonging

Diversity

Diversity goes beyond gender and race to include various dimensions, such as neurodiversity, socioeconomic status, age, sexual identity, generation, disability, veteran status, geography, and remote/in-office status.

Most organizations have improved at creating more diverse workplaces. However, without an equally important sense of equity, inclusion, and belonging, they won't realize the benefits found by Harvard Business School, including 5x higher performance, 87% better decision-making, and more innovation.

Equity

Equality gives everyone equal access to opportunities, but equity considers where each person started and focuses on ensuring the processes and policies work well for all.

Inclusion and Belonging

Belonging is a result of an inclusive environment. Harvard Business Review found high workplace belonging linked to a 56% increase in job performance, a 50% decrease in turnover risk, and a 75% reduction in sick days.

Employees with a higher sense of belonging showed a 167% increase in their employer net promoter score; their willingness to recommend their company to others.

Great Place to Work describes belonging as an employee's sense that their uniqueness is accepted and treasured by their organization and colleagues. Employees who feel treated as an "insider" feel a high level of belonging.

Inconsistent Experiences

Much of the belonging gap stems from inconsistent experiences at work. Women and underrepresented employees often have a fundamentally different experience than their white, male, cisgender colleagues.

Workplace norms remain largely rooted in the masculine defaults and white professional standards of the Mad Men era — built around an "ideal worker" who could prioritize the employer above all else because someone at home was handling everything else.

Women now make up half the workforce, yet caregiving responsibilities still fall disproportionately on them. The result is a quiet but consequential bias: women who can't stay late or attend after-work events are read as less committed — when in reality they're simply carrying more outside the office.

What's rarely acknowledged is that many return home to a second shift, the consequences of which show up as lower wages, career barriers, and discrimination.

Research shows women and people of color must demonstrate greater competence before winning promotions. And when they do rise, they're disproportionately handed "glass cliff" assignments: high-risk roles that carry a greater chance of failure because they're given problems no one before them could solve.

When Christine Lagarde was appointed to lead the IMF during the 2011 financial crisis, she captured the dynamic plainly: "Whenever the situation is really bad, you call in the woman."

The danger, of course, is that when the woman fails, it becomes easy to dismiss the next qualified woman who comes along.

Members of minority communities face their own parallel challenges. African Americans continue to navigate both explicit and implicit racism, including microaggressions — the kind of casual assumption that mistakes a Black female executive for a secretary.

To avoid such moments, many people from minority backgrounds employ code-switching: adjusting their speech, appearance, or behavior to fit in and make others more comfortable:

- A Black woman may not wear her hair naturally.

- A transgender person may feel compelled to dress a certain way.

- A white woman may reach for sports metaphors in male-dominated rooms.

These adjustments carry real costs — psychological, cognitive, and professional. The energy spent concealing one's true self is energy unavailable for the actual work.

Generational diversity adds yet another layer. For the first time in history, five generations now share the workforce — each shaped by distinct lived experiences and expectations.

Here's a Quick Overview:

Traditionalists (born between 1925 and 1945)

- Dependable, straightforward, tactful, and loyal.

- Shaped by the Great Depression, World War II, radio, and movies.

- Motivated by respect, recognition, and providing value to the company.

- Communication: personal touch, handwritten notes.

- Worldview: obedience over individualism, age = seniority, hierarchy.

- Believe employers should provide satisfying work, opportunities to contribute, and emphasize stability.

Baby Boomers (born between 1946 and 1964)

- Optimistic, competitive, workaholic, team-oriented, trade their loyalty for security.

- Shaped by the Vietnam War, Civil Rights Movement, and Watergate.

- Motivated by company loyalty, teamwork, and duty.

- Communication: phone calls and face-to-face.

- Worldview: achievement comes from paying one's dues and sacrificing for success.

- Believe employers should provide specific goals and deadlines, put them in mentor roles, and offer coaching-style feedback.

Gen X (born between 1965 and 1980)

- Flexible, informal, skeptical, and independent.

- Shaped by the AIDS epidemic, the fall of the Berlin Wall, and the dot-com boom.

- Motivated by diversity, work-life balance, and paycheck size.

- Communication: phone calls and face-to-face.

- Worldview: favor diversity; quick to move on if an employer fails to meet their needs; loyal to boss/manager.

- Believe employers should give feedback, provide flexible work arrangements and work-life balance.

Millennials (born between 1981 and 2000)

- Competitive, civic-minded, diversity, and achievement-oriented.

- Shaped by 9/11, the internet, and seeing parents laid off. Motivated by responsibility, the quality of their manager, and unique work experiences.

- Communication: IMs, texts, and email.

- Worldview: seeks challenges, growth, and development; work-life balance; loyal to their peer group.

- Believe employers should get to know them, manage by results, provide flexible work and immediate feedback.

Gen Z (born between 2001 and 2020)

- Global, entrepreneurial, progressive, and less focused on traditional work.

- Shaped by life post-9/11, the Great Recession, school shootings, and access to technology from a youth.

- Motivated by diversity, personalization, individuality, and purpose.

- Communication: IMs, texts, and social media.

- Worldview: value independence and individuality; prefer Millennial managers, innovative co-workers, and new technologies.

- Believe employers should offer a portfolio of projects, work-life balance, and allow them to be self-directed and independent.

A lesser-discussed and equally important segment of the workforce are Native Analogs and Native Digitals. As futurist and marketing thought leader Christopher Lochhead put it, there are two types of people alive today: Native Analogs (those who are Gen X and older), and Native Digitals (those who are Millennials and younger).

- Native Analogs grew up when technology was an addition to—or in some cases, a distraction from—their real lives.

- Native Digitals have grown up in a time where their "real" lives are a distraction from their (primary) digital lives. This is why they spend so much time on their phones and other screens.

Lochhead illustrates this in how both groups describe a Zoom call. Native Analogs will say, "We had a video meeting," and Native Digitals will say, "We had an in-person meeting." So, when leaders say they need everyone to come back to work in the office, it doesn't connect with Native Digitals because they think of work as a digital space, not a physical place.

- The analog American dream encompasses the belief in upward mobility through hard work, determination, owning a home, securing a stable job, and achieving financial success. It's rooted in the tangible, physical world, emphasizing material possessions, physical assets, and conventional markers of success like titles, a pension (which no longer exists), and having lots of direct reports.

- The digital American dream, on the other hand, reflects the evolving landscape of the modern era, where the digital realm plays a prominent role. Such digital success includes building a successful online business, creating a popular blog, cultivating a strong social media following, or gaining recognition in the digital sphere. The digital American dream prioritizes flexibility, creativity, and innovation over traditional notions of stability and ownership. It represents a shift toward a more digital-centric and interconnected world, where individuals can carve out their own path to success beyond the confines of traditional structures.

Understanding which dream your people are living—and designing your talent practices accordingly—is a competitive advantage most organizations have yet to unlock.

Building a More Inclusive Organization

Many organizations struggle with inclusion because they think the solution is simply a program. However, a program is by definition finite. Inclusion is a practice. It's about being inclusive in everything you do.

Many barriers to inclusion are often deeply rooted in business culture. Systematic biases can manifest subtly, such as leadership's lack of support for diversity and inclusion initiatives or unconscious bias around work assignments, performance appraisals, promotions, and compensation.

A truly inclusive workplace implements systems that minimize conscious and unconscious bias so everyone feels valued, respected, and accepted for their uniqueness. Celebrating everyone's differences signals their unique contribution to the organization.

PwC has been on this journey. A few years ago, Tim Ryan, the Senior Partner and Chairman, decided to shut down the firm for a day and hold a companywide conversation about race. The event was groundbreaking, and out of it came many things, including the creation of CEO Action for Diversity, the largest CEO-driven business commitment to advance DEI in the workplace.

It started with 150 companies committing to diversify their workforces and share best practices, and as of 2023, over 2,500 CEOs have joined. PwC is one of the few companies to publicly release its diversity data. When the firm looked at the teams that were servicing their top clients, they realized they were all white men.

They wanted to change that by investing more in their pipeline and making sponsorship a larger focus. In addition to focusing on increasing their pipeline of both female and racially/ethnically diverse partners, they are focused on building a more inclusive mindset across the firm.

This includes adding an inclusive mindset badge to the upskilling program aimed to help all PwC professionals build and practice the behaviors critical to bringing out the best in their colleagues.

Practical Ways to Do It

First and foremost, organizations must create a workplace where everyone feels respected, welcomed, valued, and included by their colleagues and superiors, regardless of their backgrounds or viewpoints.

Inclusion is about making people feel comfortable contributing and valued for their participation while feeling free to be authentic. When these criteria are met, inclusive cultures can leverage their workforce's diverse experiences, perspectives, and ideas to drive customer engagement and business results.

Embrace Flexible and Remote Work

Flexible work arrangements have emerged as a powerful tool to promote inclusivity in the workplace, particularly for underrepresented groups. Data from Future Forum in 2022 confirmed that flexible work can be a game-changer for these groups, significantly improving their sense of belonging and overall well-being.

According to the report, Black workers working from home reported a staggering 51% increase in their sense of workplace belonging and a 64% increase in their ability to manage stress. 83% of Black respondents indicated a preference for either a fully remote or hybrid workplace.

Given these compelling findings, it's clear that flexible work arrangements are crucial for creating a truly inclusive and supportive work environment.

Measure and Report

Best-in-class companies go beyond simply stating their diversity, equity, and inclusion (DEI) values and ensure their people, policies, and processes reflect them. Nike sets an example by publishing their DEI goals internally and externally and reporting quarterly on their progress. Their website showcases, in real time, how they are tracking toward these important metrics.

Cultivate a Culture of Inclusion

Creating a culture of inclusion is essential for attracting top talent — and it's rarer than most organizations think. I worked with a high-growth tech unicorn that got it right.

Despite employees spanning vastly different backgrounds — race, age, location, education, career history, and work style — the prevailing culture was one of genuine curiosity. Differences were never a point of contention. When colleagues shared their weekends — dinner parties, fishing trips, ultra-marathons, Dungeons & Dragons — nobody judged. Everyone leaned in and asked more.

Scale Micro-Affirmations

Trust and belonging are built in small moments: mirroring the language someone uses to describe their identity; drawing in those who've gone quiet; acknowledging expertise and contributions publicly; and sending the belonging cues — eye contact, attentiveness, body language — that tell someone, beneath all the noise: you are seen. You belong. You have a future here.

Micro-affirmations are not just nice to have. Research shows that social exclusion activates the same neural pathways as physical pain. Conversely, being genuinely noticed, affirmed, and included releases the brain chemistry associated with safety, trust, and motivation.

This means that the daily act of noticing someone—of remembering their name, of amplifying their idea in a meeting, of thanking them specifically for what they contributed—has measurable effects on engagement, performance, and retention. Inclusion is not a program. It is practiced person by person, moment by moment.

Embed Inclusion Into the Fabric of the Organization

Policies and statements are table stakes. Real inclusion requires identifying and addressing the biases baked into culture itself — in how decisions get made, who gets heard, and what behavior gets excused.

Leaders set the tone. That means practicing inclusive language, calling out bad behavior without making it personal, and being willing to apologize when they get it wrong — then visibly committing to doing better.

One client I worked with took this seriously from day one. Onboarding introduced diversity across more than twenty dimensions, not as a compliance exercise but as a core value woven into every practice and program.

Virtual reality simulations gave employees visceral insight into unconscious bias and privilege — the kind of understanding that a slide deck simply can't produce.

Provide Cross-Mentoring and Leadership Team Support

Cross-mentoring programs are one of the most effective ways to achieve insight into your constituencies, ensuring that you stay ahead of the curve in an ever-changing world.

Another powerful strategy for gaining diverse perspectives and ensuring that you view everything through an inclusion lens is rotating leaders of employee resource groups (ERGs) onto the leadership team.

By bringing in people from different backgrounds: women, people of color, younger employees, you can avoid major blind spots and gain new insights that will keep you competitive and innovative.

Leaders Role-Model Inclusive Behaviors

The behavior of executives and managers can make or break an organization's efforts to create an inclusive workplace. According to Deloitte, it can make a 70% difference in the proportion of diverse employees who feel included versus those who do not.

That's why senior leadership teams must lead by example and hold all levels of management accountable for fostering inclusive environments that support all employees.

Carla Harris, a bestselling author and senior leader at Morgan Stanley, suggests a simple way for leaders to start being more inclusive is by initiating a conversation with their team: "I'll go first, not because I believe I'm the most knowledgeable, but because of my seniority. Then, Sally, I invite you to contribute. Following that, Bill, I encourage you to expand on Sally's ideas, and Shonda, could you provide a contrasting perspective as the devil's advocate?"

This approach acknowledges and includes everyone, inviting them to share their thoughts, fostering ownership of the outcome, and encouraging both leaders and team members to challenge one another openly.

Chapter 8

The King Has Been Dethroned

We're amidst a fundamental shift in leadership. In today's rapidly evolving world, only 23% of organizations believe that their leaders possess the necessary skills to navigate the new landscape, according to the latest Deloitte Global Human Capital Trends report.

The divide between leaders and their employees continues to widen, due to outdated perspectives on work and a growing gap in lived experiences between the C-suite and employees.

A great example is Future Forum data showing most executives expect their employees to come to the office at least three days a week, whereas less than a quarter of employees share this preference.

This exemplifies the disconnect that has emerged between leaders and employees, with many executives failing to understand their workforce's changing needs and expectations.

To truly excel in this new world, leaders must embrace a fresh set of fundamentals and harness the perspectives and full potential of their employees in innovative ways.

New Rules of Engagement

To the dismay of old-school leaders who live and die by the command and control approach, the role of a leader today is no longer about basking in the glory at the top while the "minions" do the work.

Today's workforce will not bow down to the hierarchy and are not impressed by the aggressive alpha male CEO of the 1980s.

Today's employee has more access to information and influence than past generations. They have been raised as leaders themselves, being consulted by parents and influencing peers on a large scale via social media since they got their first phone.

This means a different approach to leadership is needed. As my favorite executive coach, Marshall Goldsmith, says, "What got you here won't get you there."

The only way to lead effectively when you can't force people to follow is to provide context, be a role model, and lead from a place of shared goals.

The very language of leadership has transformed, with empathy, authenticity, and the ability to enable others now taking center stage.

Today's leaders must be able to connect with their team members on a deeper level, showing genuine concern for their well-being and creating an environment where everyone can thrive. Authenticity is also essential, as employees quickly detect insincerity or lack of integrity.

Perhaps the most important skill for leaders in this new era is the ability to facilitate the greatness of others. Leaders must create opportunities for employees to showcase their strengths, encourage them to take on new challenges, and provide the support and resources they need to succeed.

Lead Yourself First

As the great philosopher Seneca once said, "No one is fit to rule who is not master of themselves." Many of the issues we're facing today could be resolved if those in charge could better manage themselves.

Think back to the great leaders you've encountered. What sets them apart? More often than not, their success can be traced back to their ability to lead themselves with mastery.

Great leaders understand leadership starts from within. They know that to lead others effectively, they must first lead themselves. They prioritize self-care, self-alignment, and intention. They make it a point to deeply understand their strengths, weaknesses, values, and emotions.

This foundation is critical to effectively leading anyone, as we cannot give to others what we do not possess ourselves.

We must fill our own cup first if we want to inspire, elicit greatness, and hold space for others.

Success is built on basic, boring, high-leverage habits like optimal sleep, healthy eating, regular exercise, and morning routines. Jeff Bezos, for example, prioritizes his sleep and only schedules mentally strenuous meetings before lunch.

For some, it means having mindfulness, meditation, and gratitude practices, which can enhance intentionality and effectiveness. Something as simple as checking in with yourself throughout the day and asking, "Who am I being right now?" is a powerful question that reminds you that you have a choice in how you show up at every moment.

Stay centered by staying aligned with your values, as Bill George, former CEO of Medtronic, and Hubert Joly, former CEO of Best Buy, emphasize. Without a clear understanding of what you stand for, it's impossible to chart a course or know why you're heading in a certain direction.

Shockingly, 60% of leaders say they don't know their core values. If this is you, start with human behavior expert Dr. John Demartini's values determination exercise.

There is a lot of data on the effectiveness of strategic reflection and journaling. Journaling about gratitude shifts you into a long-term perspective, enabling you to overcome short-term thinking.

A masterful leader demonstrates self-control, discipline, and emotional intelligence. They manage their thoughts, emotions, and actions with mindfulness and purpose, making decisions based on sound judgment, rationality, and the long view rather than being driven by impulses or external pressures.

In her bestselling book, *The Long Game: How to Be a Long-Term Thinker in a Short-Term World*, Dorie Clark highlights the importance of taking the long view, even if there's a short-term cost. She says most CEOs say they support the issues in the public zeitgeist, but many don't stand up publicly to support them because they're too worried about the short-term shareholder response.

This short-term thinking stops them from doing the right thing and using their power to take a stand. Whereas, taking a long-term perspective, and asking what the long-term impact of taking a position on one of these issues might be, could yield greater results.

Paul Polman demonstrated this as CEO of Unilever by eliminating quarterly reporting to the board and shareholders — recognizing that short-term accountability cycles were incompatible with long-term strategic thinking. Despite shareholder pushback, he didn't blink.

To truly grow as a leader, it's essential to seek guidance and feedback from those outside of your usual circle. Consider enlisting the help of a top-notch executive or performance coach, like Wendy Rhodes from the Showtime series Billions, or leverage the proven 360-degree coaching tools of Marshall Goldsmith.

To get a fresh perspective on your ideas and behaviors, it's vital to have what Adam Grant calls a "challenge network", including devil's advocates who provide critical feedback.

A reverse mentor keeps you connected to what's actually happening on the ground and the relationship benefits both: they gain access and visibility; you gain perspective you can't get any other way.

You Are No Longer the Hero

Gone are the days when companies operated top-down, with decisions flowing from the executive suite to the field. With today's fast-paced and unpredictable business landscape, organizations need to empower their front-line workers to make their own decisions.

This is particularly crucial in the face of our volatile, uncertain, complex, and ambiguous (VUCA) world, where information and expertise need to be shared and acted upon quicker than in the past.

Giving the people on the ground the tools and authority to drive the organization forward enables companies to stay agile, responsive, and competitive while increasing the engagement of their people.

Former US Navy captain L. David Marquet is a great example of this principle. At one point, Marquet was selected to captain the USS Olympia, a nuclear-powered attack submarine. He studied for over a year to take command, working to understand every detail of the submarine's operations.

Marquet was unexpectedly diverted to take command of the USS Santa Fe instead when its captain quit. Santa Fe was the worst-performing submarine in the fleet and was a different type of submarine, which he knew little about.

Without the answers, he couldn't give commands—he quickly learned that in a situation like this, when your people have the answers and you don't, your job is to create an environment where they can do what they need to do as easily as possible.

He did this by saying, "I don't know. What do you think?" Instead of giving them orders, he asked them to tell him what they intended to do. This enabled the team members to not only come up with an approach but voluntarily commit to it, instead of Marquet telling them what to do and expecting them to comply.

The counterintuitive leadership pivot is pulling back on saving the day and, instead, focusing on being more coach-like, getting curious, asking questions, and letting your team find the answers.

This attitude expands the employee's point of view and increases their sense of agency. This is especially important for your Millennial and Gen Z employees, as they are used to being consulted by their parents on what television to buy or where they want to go on vacation, for example.

Imagine their surprise when they go to work, and their boss tells them to do something without asking about their point of view. A more effective approach is to say, "Here is the problem I want to solve. Could you come back to me with a proposal of what you recommend we do to address it?" When they feel consulted and trusted, they will employ their creativity, agency, and commitment to the problem.

Hubert Joly, the former CEO of Best Buy, understood the importance of co-creating with his people when he was brought in to turn the company around. He spent his first week in stores, listening to front-line employees and asking for their ideas.

He realized that they had all the answers, and by working together, they were able to come up with solutions he could have never seen from his vantage point.

Be a Meaning Maker

One of the most important jobs of a modern leader is to create meaning for the people in the organization. It's a powerful precursor to employee engagement, but unfortunately, research from MIT reveals that people rarely attribute meaningful work to their leaders.

Instead, they often mention the obstacles leaders put in their way, such as micromanagement, destroying a sense of achievement and connection by switching people off project teams before the work is completed, or thwarting ownership of problems and tasks by continually overriding their judgment.

In Chapter 13, we delve into several ways to create meaning across the organization, but here are a few key ways leaders can get started.

Mattering

When people feel like they and/or the work they do matters, it provides them with meaning. In *How to Create Mattering at Work,* author and meaningful work researcher Zach Mercurio, PhD says mattering involves showing people how they make a unique impact.

Managers can create this by ensuring people regularly see, hear, and feel their work's effect on teammates and customers. Instead of just saying "thank you" or "good job," it's important for managers to get more granular and show people how what they did makes a difference and why it's important. This creates meaning, while highlighting what good looks like.

Provide Context and Connect the Dots

Show employees how their work impacts the organization, the customer, the community, or the world. By doing this, you can transform the average employee's day-to-day tasks into something bigger and more meaningful.

A great, simple example of this is Gerry Anderson, the former CEO of DTE Energy. When he joined the company, they had low employee engagement and productivity. Anderson started his tenure by making a video that articulated the impact of truck drivers, operators, and other employees on customers. When he shared it with employees, many were moved to tears and applause.

Engagement scores climbed. The company received a Gallup Great Workplace award five years in a row, and DTE's stock price more than tripled during Gerry's time there.

Bring the Impact to Life

Leaders should be asking themselves, "How can we get employees closer to the impact their work has?" Bill George, the former CEO of medical device company Medtronic, did this annually at the holiday party.

Instead of the usual routine, George invited patients who had personally benefited from Medtronic's products to share their stories on stage. These real-life accounts brought the impact of employees' work to life right before their eyes and created a compelling experience where employees could see, hear, and feel the direct positive outcomes of their efforts.

Imagine the emotions that surged through the room as employees listened to patients sharing how Medtronic's pacemakers and diabetes therapies had transformed their lives. It was a powerful reminder of the significant difference their work made in the lives of real people.

Through this meaningful connection, Bill helped employees see the impact of their work. The stories ignited a sense of pride and motivation among employees, knowing their work made a tangible difference in the world.

Be a Storyteller and Recognition Dealer

Recognition, particularly non-monetary recognition, is a leader's most powerful, yet underutilized tool. Chapter 11 will look in more detail at recognizing employees and celebrating success.

As a leader, it's important to always be on the lookout for stories of exceptional performance and employees living out the organization's values and purpose. Share these stories widely, and ensure that you go beyond a simple "good job." Provide meaningful details on how the individual's unique contribution made a significant impact.

By recognizing employees in meaningful ways, you can inspire them to continue their exceptional work and feel valued for their contributions.

Carol Tomé, the CEO of UPS, for example, writes nearly two hundred letters a week recognizing different UPS employees for doing amazing things. She recently recounted a story about writing a letter to a UPS driver who, while delivering a package, observed a nearby house on fire and promptly woke up the homeowner who had been asleep.

Mentor and Develop Your People

Today's workforce is more educated, resourceful, and technologically astute than any other generation. They can quickly gather information and curate solutions from Google, YouTube, ChatGPT, and social media.

However, they lack the contextualization, critical thinking, and wisdom that come with hard-earned experience. More than any other generation, they crave mentorship and development.

This is where a leader can flip the relationship from transactional to transformational. Bonus points if you get them to cross-mentor you—we all know your TikTok skills could use an upgrade.

We discuss this in depth in Chapter 12, but an easy way to get started is to simply ask your people what they care about, understand their strengths, their interests, and where they want to grow. Ask what talents and experiences they aren't able to utilize right now that they want to, and then find ways to bridge those with what the organization needs.

Define opportunities for people to stretch their thinking and abilities by extending concrete challenges and shifting the responsibility for finding solutions to them. When I was a junior consultant, I had an amazing senior woman named Vreni mentor me. She suggested we flip roles on an engagement we were on—I would be the lead and she would be supporting me.

This unleashed a fire of motivation, strategic thinking, and bias for action in me. I knew the job was on my shoulders, and that Vreni had my back if I needed it. I was highly dedicated to taking on the role of a leader, constantly asking myself how a leader would speak, act, and engage with the client. Doing this made me not just think of myself as a leader, but act as one from then on.

This is a simple and extremely powerful way to grow your people exponentially while scaling your bandwidth.

Building Trust

The most accurate predictor of a leader's success is how much their people trust and respect them. This is critical in deciding whether to follow a leader, especially in unknown and ambiguous situations, which is our new reality.

Harvard Business School professor and trust expert Frances Frei defines trust as a three-legged stool that includes authenticity, the rigor of your logic when making decisions, and making others feel you care about them. Let's look at each of the three legs.

Harvard Business Review found in their latest Work Trend Index that 89% of employees ranked authenticity as the number-one quality a leader or manager should have.

So what does authenticity look like in practice? It starts at the top—leaders can set the tone for a culture where open, genuine, and empathetic connections can happen. You must lead by example, using an authentic voice to communicate openness and inclusivity.

Angela Ahrendts, former SVP at Apple and former CEO of Burberry, did this when she first joined Apple. The team was looking to introduce her to the organization by sending out the typical formal email announcement with a professional headshot, but she pushed back.

Instead, she suggested they film a short, candid iPhone video without any production. She even had them keep in the impromptu call from her daughter during the video. This resulted in hundreds of emails from Apple employees thanking her for showing her authentic human side.

The second leg of the trust stool comes when people trust your logic and feel you have thought through decisions that impact them. This is where sharing the "why" behind decisions, initiatives, and ways of working is powerful—because it lets people see inside your thought process, and that builds trust in your logic.

The third leg of the trust stool is caring about and showing interest in employees. Promoting trust with your people starts with seeing them as human beings rather than bullets in a job description. As Monty Moran, the former CEO of Chipotle, says, "Convey to people they are cared for, needed, empowered, and that you are curious about them, and you'll get the very best of them."

Remember, your employees are humans who work for you, not workers who happen to be human. When we know, respect, and are interested in our people as human beings, magic happens.

One of my retail clients saw this firsthand when she visited her top-performing and lowest-attrition store and met with the manager to discover the secret sauce.

It turns out, in his 1-on1s, he asked each associate, "What is your dream—at and outside of work?" Then he made it his job to help them achieve their dream. This paid off because it helped him understand what drives his people and what their struggles are, and made them feel that he respected them as human beings.

It's increasingly important for leaders to practice listening to, and learning about their people. The benefits of this are even seen on a chemical level. Active listening releases dopamine in the brain, which makes the two people like and trust each other more. This builds esteem, connection, and meaning for employees.

Research from ADP's Head of Research, People, and Performance, Marcus Buckingham, suggests organizations best build trust by empowering managers and reducing their span of responsibility so that frequent, individualized attention is possible.

Consider leveraging weekly check-ins where the manager asks questions like "What did you love about last week?" "What did you loathe?" "What are your priorities this coming week?" "How can I best help?" It doesn't matter whether the check-in is in person, by phone, by email, or in an app. What matters is that it happens.

Many organizations, such as Cisco, have instituted this as a core ritual. The data from millions of check-ins show this practice increases team members' engagement scores by 33% and reduces voluntary turnover by 13%.

Create an Abundance of Psychological Safety

No one will risk being themselves unless they trust that they won't be penalized or judged for being authentic, speaking up, or making mistakes. This is what Harvard Business School professor Amy Edmondson calls psychological safety, which was also found to be the top driver in high-performing teams.

Today, we need people to bring their full selves to work, and that's only possible when they have psychological safety—especially for employees who come from underrepresented groups and may not see themselves in the people who lead them.

Show Vulnerability

One of the quickest ways to create psychological safety and build trust is to show authentic vulnerability. Leaders who are what I call "securely vulnerable" are confident enough in themselves to demonstrate both strength and vulnerability.

As Brené Brown describes, "Vulnerability sounds like truth and feels like courage. Truth and courage aren't always comfortable, but they're never weaknesses." Leaders who embody this duality exhibit a relatability people can identify with on a human level while projecting strength and a vision that compels others to follow.

A great example is former Sprint CEO Dan Hesse, who was brought in during the Sprint/Nextel merger to turn the joint organization around while building a new culture.

He quickly ascertained that they were almost bankrupt and had about six months before the money ran out.

He decided an all-hands-on-deck approach was the only chance to save the company. So he was very vulnerable and transparent with his people about the situation, to the point where he shared a dashboard with everyone in the organization showing when the money would run out.

He was also very open about needing to cut costs and lay people off. Contrary to what you may think, this caused engagement scores to go up because he was transparent and co-created solutions with them.

Sprint went from last place in the wireless industry in customer satisfaction to first. He has been recognized with the Corporate Responsibility Lifetime Achievement Award, is a Top Rated CEO on Glassdoor, and is one of five Best Turnaround CEOs of all time, among other honors.

Celebrate the Messenger

When someone steps forward with bad news or a "failure," leaders should show appreciation and respect for taking risks and focus on what the team can learn from it.

When Alan Mulally first became Ford's CEO, no one on the senior ops team dared admit there was any problem for fear of being fired—even though the car manufacturer was in serious trouble.

When someone finally spoke up in a meeting, asking for help solving a manufacturing issue, Mulally clapped, signaling to the team that asking for help was safe and encouraged.

Pink Elephants and Silent Problems

A good way to do this is asking people to list all the issues being avoided. Remind them that, as a team, you can only solve the problems that are made explicit. Then instead of finding a single person to fix it, turn the issue into a collective problem to solve.

The Elevated Role of the Manager

Over the past few years, the role of the manager has undergone a significant transformation, from an agent of surveillance and control, to a pivotal force that needs to be strategically equipped to effectively navigate the complexities of our rapidly changing world.

There are mountains of data showing people don't quit jobs—they quit bosses. Gallup research shows how crucial great management is: 70% of employee engagement is attributed to the manager, and $360 billion in losses occur due to bad leadership each year.

Elevating the skills of managers is a critical step organizations cannot afford to overlook. While Chapter 12 will go in-depth on innovative ways to grow and develop all employees, here are a few specific to supporting managers.

Peer-to-Peer Coaching

Many organizations don't develop their managers, but even those who do often miss a critical piece. While online learning, instructor-led training, assessments, coaching, and 360 feedback have value, they don't address the uniquely isolating role of the manager.

With pressures coming at them from above and below, managers often feel they have nowhere to turn for support that feels safe and accessible. Enter the power of peer-to-peer coaching.

Companies from Zillow to Goldman Sachs to Boston Scientific use a peer-to-peer coaching platform called

Imperative to empower managers to support and learn from each other.

With Imperative, managers are matched with each other every quarter for guided coaching conversations over video. Over the year, they are matched with 4 other managers, creating a trusted network of peers. Neither person is the "teacher" or "student." The structured format enables participants to help each other process the emotional roller coaster of people management, normalize their challenges, and find solutions.

Let Them Try It On

A while back, I worked with a mid-sized technology firm to develop what became a very successful manager accelerator program. The program allowed people to try out being a manager for six months before officially stepping into the role.

When applying to the program, the individual was asked to discuss why they wanted to be a manager, what they hoped to accomplish with the experience, and how they wanted to serve their team as a leader.

The program included shadowing, snackable digital training materials, and an ongoing 360 feedback framework. This ensured those who went on to the manager role were first able to demonstrate that they had the right intentions, experience, and skills to be successful.

There was no penalty for those who tried it on and realized it wasn't the best fit. After six months, these folks returned to their previous role or found another one.

Community

One of my clients found it extremely helpful to take a community-building perspective by creating a manager mastermind group and a Slack channel to unite managers from different teams, organizations, and industries.

It provides an innovative central hub for exchanging invaluable resources, addressing pressing questions, discussing common pain points, and sharing game-changing tips. They also found that the channel serves as a wellspring of networking and innovation, generating fresh ideas that benefit individual managers and their respective organizations.

Now that we've looked at the evolving, yet pivotal role of leadership in the new world of work, the next several chapters will look at ways organizations can cultivate and harness intrinsic motivation and high performance by meeting employees' human needs.

The two leading theories that explore the relationship between human needs, motivation, and performance are Self-Determination Theory and Maslow's Hierarchy of Needs.

Psychologists Richard Ryan and Edward Deci developed the Self-Determination Theory, which posits that human motivation, well-being, and performance are enhanced when individuals have a sense of autonomy, competence, and relatedness in their actions and relationships. When any of these three psychological needs is unsupported or thwarted, it will have a detrimental effect—as Daniel Pink discusses in Drive.

Maslow's Hierarchy of Needs theory states that humans are motivated by certain physiological and psychological needs, and when they are unmet and/or stifled, people become demotivated and disengaged.

In a work context, this means it's critical to meet survival needs such as physical and mental safety and well-being as table stakes. Once this is accomplished, people can focus on satisfying higher needs such as belonging, connection, self-worth, esteem, growth, meaning, and purpose.

As mentioned in Chapter 4, the majority of organizations not only fail to fulfill these needs but unintentionally suppress them—which is the underlying cause of the widespread epidemic of dissatisfaction and disengagement at work.

Organizations that tap into the very essence of what makes us human, and progress from frustrating employee needs to addressing them, have the power to create a transformative impact on their people, the business, and perhaps the world.

Chapter 9

The Foundation of High Performance

At the bottom of Maslow's hierarchy of human needs lie survival and safety. Deloitte research shows that when these needs, defined holistically as financial, mental, and physical wellbeing, are not met, employee engagement and productivity decline, and attrition and healthcare costs skyrocket.

Financial Wellbeing

Ensuring employees have some level of financial wellbeing is critical. If people are worried about layoffs or are making trade-offs between paying their rent and going to the doctor, there is no way they can give the best of themselves at work.

A 2017 study found 72% of Americans ranked finances as their top source of stress.

A 2022 Financial Times study found that financially stressed workers cost companies $40 billion annually due to higher turnover, lower productivity, lower engagement, and higher absenteeism. The study also found that while most organizations agree financial wellbeing is necessary, only about 20% confirm they are paying living wages to all employees.

PayPal is a great example of an organization that got creative in addressing financial wellbeing, and as a result, it grew its profits by 25%.

Several years ago, PayPal CEO Dan Schulman learned that many of his lowest-paid employees were barely making enough to survive.

To address the root cause of this, he took a strategic, data-driven approach to measure the financial health of their employees and created a metric: "net disposable income," or NDI. NDI went beyond the fair market price and measured how much money people had after they paid their taxes and essential living expenses.

From there, PayPal created a four-part financial wellness program for its lower-paid employees. It included raising the wages for employees with low NDIs and providing every employee, including entry-level ones, an opportunity to own stock in the company. Next, they rolled out a comprehensive financial literacy program for employees.

In their research, PayPal also found healthcare costs were consuming a large chunk of their people's NDI, and as a result, Schulman lowered healthcare costs by 60% for the company's lowest-paid employees.

This cost PayPal tens of millions of dollars, but Schulman insists that the expense was worth it.

In the months after the program began, customer satisfaction ticked up, employees were more engaged, and PayPal's stock continued to soar.

Innovative software firm, Tanium, has also made financial well-being a priority. They equip their team members with the knowledge and resources necessary to make informed financial decisions.

Through regular financial wellness weeks, employees have access to a wealth of valuable resources, including information sessions, one-on-one financial advising, and on-demand financial tools.

Mental and Physical Wellbeing

Research shows companies with employees who have high levels of mental and physical wellbeing see nearly 25% more profits than their Fortune 500 counterparts who don't.

Unfortunately, poor employee health costs employers almost $300 billion and 1.5 million days of lost productivity, according to the Integrated Benefits Institute.

A 2017 Deloitte Wellbeing at Work study found most employees say their health has worsened or stayed the same over the last year. 70% of them say workloads, job stress, and long hours are getting in the way of their health, with 40% of employees and 75% of the C-suite seriously considering quitting for a job that would better support their well-being.

When it comes to mental and physical well-being, unfortunately, most workplaces not only don't contribute to it but stifle it.

As someone who began her career as a workplace productivity and well-being researcher, I have seen firsthand the impact workplace practices and lifestyle can have on wellbeing.

The top contributors to low productivity, low engagement, absenteeism, burnout, and high healthcare costs are related to stress, anxiety, poor diet, sedentary lifestyles, and lack of sleep. Much of this is exacerbated by the ways we work.

At a minimum, we need to reverse this relationship to ensure work is not contributing to a decline in wellbeing. But we can do better. If we want our people and organizations to flourish, we must implement practices that enrich wellbeing.

Interventions such as on-site farmers markets, nutrition classes, referrals to dietitians, meditation rooms, encouraging the use of stairs and walking paths, taking walking meetings, on-site fitness centers, and discounted gym memberships are shown to promote wellbeing and increase productivity.

Equally important is providing dedicated time for employees, both during and outside of working hours, to integrate wellbeing activities. This allows them to recharge and attain a healthier work-life balance.

Poor mental health among employees is directly linked to higher turnover rates, substance abuse, absenteeism, higher healthcare costs, lower productivity, and lower engagement.

The latest report from US Surgeon General Vivek Murthy on workplace health and wellbeing discusses the harmful effects of stress, such as sleep disruption, impaired metabolism, high blood pressure, high cholesterol, heart disease, obesity, cancer, autoimmune diseases, depression, anxiety, suicidal thoughts, and substance misuse.

It's clear that the repercussions of stress are far-reaching and have the potential to wreak havoc on our physical and mental health, and as a result, our organizations.

Post-pandemic, many organizations have recognized the importance of mental wellbeing and are stepping up their support.

American Express, for example, supports employees on their mental health journeys through its "Here for You. Here for Each Other" program. It includes webinars, shared tools, and talking points for leaders to help with difficult conversations to ensure everyone knows it's okay not to be okay and to ask for help.

The more progressive organizations have therapists and coaches on staff or, at minimum, a budget for employees to go on their own. Think about how much this could free up managers, who have increasingly assumed the additional role of therapist and coach.

Taking on these additional responsibilities has led to feelings of overwhelm and excessive strain for managers. Having dedicated and appropriately trained resources to handle these roles instead would bring significant benefits.

One of my clients has well-being coaches who partner with employees to create a personalized wellness strategy to proactively plan for well-being.

The company also offers a safe space to discuss specific needs, such as navigating difficult one-on-one conversations with their teams. This has improved self-awareness and the effectiveness of the team's interactions.

We have to address burnout. As technology advances, employees face increasing demands to be constantly available, perform at a superhuman level, and provide discretionary effort as a baseline. However, this unsustainable pace leads to burnout, disengagement, and attrition.

A Deloitte study found that 77% of individuals report experiencing burnout due to factors such as unrealistic expectations, long hours, and lack of recognition. Almost half of Millennials leave their jobs due to those factors, and it costs $125 billion annually.

Unlike work of previous eras, knowledge work today requires innovation, analytical thinking, and high levels of emotional intelligence. It also means work often doesn't stop at five o'clock.

This shift requires increased flexibility and boundaries to enable workers to recharge, keep their minds sharp, and sustain energy levels for the long term. Monthly refresh days, no-meeting Fridays, and parameters around sending emails only during core business hours can help with this.

Other factors contributing to burnout include friction (discussed in Chapter 14), such as redundant processes, clunky technology, micromanagement, toxic cultures, exclusion, and a lack of meaning in the work.

On the back of the 2022 US Surgeon General's report highlighting the growth rates and impacts of burnout in the workplace, the Australian government announced new workplace regulations to reduce the risk of three psychosocial hazards, including lack of role clarity, inadequate recognition, and poor support.

Gallup reports that reducing these hazards leads to improved engagement, increased wellbeing, and more productive and profitable organizations.

Employees say flexible work, wellbeing programs, and paid time off for recovery and mental health would prevent or alleviate burnout.

It's also important for colleagues and managers to model boundary-setting behavior and share stories about their personal wellbeing practices to prevent burnout.

One of my healthcare clients has a peer support program that connects employees with a trained peer responder when they need to talk about a particularly challenging work experience. This program alone has increased engagement scores and retention of their nurses.

Leverage biochemistry to increase employee wellbeing. Dr. Paul Zak's research has shown that reducing cortisol, known as the stress chemical, while increasing oxytocin, serotonin, and dopamine can create a positive impact on trust, connection, and belonging.

So how can leaders achieve this? Reducing micromanagement and combative discussions, and increasing transparency can lower cortisol levels.

Additionally, giving employees more autonomy can increase their sense of trust, which releases oxytocin, the bonding chemical. To increase serotonin, leaders can focus on promoting social connection and managing stress levels.

Finally, activating the seeking system or ventral striatum, which releases dopamine, can lead to intrinsic motivation, enjoyment, and better performance. Leaders can activate this system by encouraging employees to learn, experiment, and explore.

They can help employees leverage their strengths and give employees information about the why behind their work, including how it impacts others and the organization's goals.

Studies have shown that simply thinking about one's impact on others or directly helping someone else can boost the happiness trifecta of oxytocin, dopamine, and serotonin.

If we are deliberate, we can create regenerative workplaces that function as engines for health and wellbeing. We have an unprecedented opportunity to examine the role of work in our lives and explore ways to better enable all workers to thrive both within and beyond the workplace.

Meeting these fundamental well-being needs enables employees to focus their energy on increasing their fulfillment and delivering high performance at work.

Organizations that make well-being a genuine strategic priority—not a wellness program bolted on to an otherwise unhealthy environment—see remarkable returns.

The research is unambiguous: wellbeing and performance are not in tension. They are mutually reinforcing.

When people feel physically healthy, financially secure, and mentally resourced, they can bring their full selves to the work.

When the work itself depletes those resources, no amount of yoga subsidies or mindfulness apps will fix it.

The goal is to design the environment so that work actively contributes to flourishing, rather than fighting against it.

Chapter 10

Connection and Community

A recent Harvard Business Review study showed 65% of people don't feel any sense of connection or community at work. However, those who do are 58% more likely to thrive, 55% more likely to be engaged, and 66% more likely to stay with the organization. Loneliness costs the US economy over $406 billion a year.

From the time we are born, we are looking for connection. As Dan and Chip Heath note in their book The Power of Moments, connection is built on feelings of unity, empathy, and validation. It's about being seen, understood, and accepted as a fellow human.

Many people say building meaningful relationships at work is a major challenge. It's not always clear who to connect with, how to initiate those connections, or where to find like-minded colleagues. And even when we do make the leap, there's often a lack of psychological safety that holds us back from truly opening up and forming deep bonds.

Fortunately, there are things companies can do to help their employees cultivate the relationships they need to succeed.

Noticing as a Bridge to Connection

Creating authentic connections is essential for building a positive and productive workplace. It all starts with noticing people as individuals and valuing their unique qualities. Shockingly, nearly half of employees report feeling unnoticed.

I once mentored a young woman who landed a dream job at a prominent creative firm. She enjoyed her work, liked her colleagues, and was compensated well. But despite all of this, she confided in me a month in that she was considering leaving the company.

Why? Because she felt unimportant to her boss. He repeatedly misspelled and mispronounced her name, even after being corrected several times. His lack of attention to the basics mitigated the many positive aspects of the job, and she ended up leaving soon after.

In *How to Create Mattering at Work,* author and meaningful work researcher Zach Mercurio, PhD writes that "Noticing others is the deliberate act of seeing someone's uniqueness, paying attention to the ebbs and flows of their lives, and taking action to show them you see and hear them."

Managers can do this through regular check-ins with employees focusing on their personal lives, stress levels, and work struggles. Simply changing surface-level questions like

"How are you?" to questions like "What's giving you energy this week?" or "What's taking energy from you this week?" or "What can I do to support you?" can give the leader more insight into people's lives.

When you pay attention to the highs and lows of someone's life and show them you hear and understand them, you're building the foundation for genuine connection.

By employing a few simple practices and skills, individuals—regardless of whether they lead people or not—can make others feel seen and valued.

Take note of important events and milestones in people's lives and follow up with them. Remembering someone's favorite snack or asking how they're doing after an illness can make all the difference. And when someone is absent, let them know that they were missed. Incorporating these practices will help people feel seen, appreciated, and more engaged in their work.

Cultivating Connection

Creating connections within teams and across an organization is more than just a nice-to-have—it's essential for success. Aaron Hurst is the founder of Imperative, an enterprise platform specifically designed to foster meaningful conversations that accelerate trust between people.

Their data shows after just three conversations on the platform, 87% of employees report that they have built a meaningful relationship they plan to sustain.

Hurst explains that fostering connections and building social capital improves collaboration, engagement, and agility. But how do we cultivate these connections? Hurst advocates for meaningful conversations that promote mutual understanding and validation.

By actively listening and sharing stories and challenges, individuals can create trust and empathy that transcend traditional workplace relationships. Hurst suggests that organizations should facilitate connections among their employees based on shared interests or identities, such as manager training, onboarding, or employee resource groups.

Neuroscience backs up this approach, showing that when we see someone as "like me" in some way, our brains release oxytocin, the bonding chemical that strengthens relationships. By intentionally creating connections and building social capital, we can unlock the full potential of our teams and organizations.

Digital platforms like Imperative can be powerful tools for building connections and trust within teams. Another excellent tool is the Café app, which connects team members based on shared interests in events, groups, and communities.

Leaders who intentionally create opportunities for shared experiences, challenges, and purpose can ignite a powerful sense of connection among team members. When people feel connected to one another, they're more likely to collaborate, be creative, and drive innovation.

All-hands meetings, offsites, and bonding events are just a few examples of activities that can help team members feel a sense of togetherness when done well. From renting out a museum to working together on a volunteer activity for charity to hosting a Tony Robbins-style fire-walking session, there are countless ways to create memorable shared experiences that strengthen bonds.

There are plenty of opportunities to do this for distributed teams too. During the pandemic, several clients of mine held virtual offsites with interesting speakers, scavenger hunts, and show-and-tell sessions. It can be as simple as having the team listen to a specific podcast, read a book, or try a recipe, and then discuss it together. These are all great ways to foster commonality.

As a leader, it's up to you to intentionally design team interactions that bring people together and encourage a sense of community.

The Power of Uniting People Toward a Shared Goal

When people work toward a shared purpose, a sense of belonging and pride ignites within them, driving them to go above and beyond to achieve the objectives. The synergy of everyone's unique skills, perspectives, and talents working in unison toward a shared vision is a force to be reckoned with.

Think of a championship sports team or a high-performing emergency room team, who unites around a common mission. Their ego and focus on themselves drop away, enabling them to perform at higher levels to contribute to the collective.

To cultivate this kind of energy in your organization, you can frame things in a way that inspires people emotionally and encourages them to unite around a common goal.

Creating communities where people can take ownership and feel a sense of belonging is an excellent way to do this. When people come together in a peer-to-peer community, they support each other, help solve problems, and hold each other accountable.

Employee resource groups (ERGs) are great examples of this, bringing people together around shared values, interests, and commonalities. Leveraging the power of community to tackle a particular problem or initiative can also create a sense of belonging and purpose while scaling a mission across the organization.

Building social connections like this that make employees feel valued can create trusted work relationships that mitigate burnout, reduce turnover, and contribute to well-being at scale.

One of my clients was a hospital system that was experiencing high levels of burnout and turnover among nurses coming out of the pandemic.

So we designed an intervention where, each week, the nurses would receive an email featuring a story of another nurse's experience at work. These emails also included a prompt to encourage nurses to reflect on their own experiences, in hopes that they would share positive stories their co-workers might relate to.

The stories were collected and stored in an online database for future emails. Through sharing stories, the nurses could highlight the challenges of the job, find commonality, and support their peers. The emails fostered a greater sense of belonging, support, and professional identity, as more nurses were able to empathize with the stories and challenges shared by their colleagues.

After a few months, we measured burnout and turnover again and found a 5% decrease in burnout and a 47% reduction in turnover.

Cultivating respectful relationships where people feel valued contributes to feelings of self-worth, competence, and a sense of dignity at work. This is foundational to high performance, accountability, and increased collaboration.

The ROI of connection is real, even if it's harder to put on a balance sheet than a software platform.

Organizations that invest in creating genuine human bonds among their people—through deliberate rituals, shared experiences, leader behavior, and tools that facilitate meaningful interaction—build something their competitors cannot easily replicate: a community.

And communities, as history has repeatedly shown, are far more resilient, innovative, and enduring than any collection of isolated individuals working in parallel ever can be.

Chapter 11

Treat People Like Adults

As we journey through life, we generally experience a growing sense of independence and the ability to make choices about how we allocate our time, where we invest our efforts, and the identities we embrace.

However, when we transition to the working world, we often find ourselves confined to fixed working hours, a specific workplace location, rigid procedures, and roles dictated by tradition. This is where many workplace issues stem from.

Two of our most fundamental needs as adult humans are autonomy and agency. The need to feel in control of our lives, to make decisions, and to be able to take action is essential to our sense of self, motivation, and well-being.

Yet, in the workplace, these vital needs are often stifled by the suffocating grip of old mindsets, hierarchy, bureaucracy, and micromanagement. The result? Decreased agility, productivity, engagement, and commitment.

According to neuroscientist Dr. David Rock, employees who lack autonomy and agency lose their sense of purpose and drive. As he says, "When nothing feels in your control, why even try?" This state of learned helplessness leads to passivity and reduced performance.

The good news is that organizations can turn this around by giving their employees more autonomy wherever possible. By providing flexibility in terms of where or when they work, giving them a say in how decisions are made, and soliciting feedback, employees feel empowered to take more control of their work.

Autonomy and Agency

Employees who feel like they have the power to make a difference have what psychologists call an internal locus of control, which translates into a higher sense of ownership and engagement.

A great example of this is the Ritz-Carlton's "$2,000 rule." The co-founder and first president, Horst Schulze, created a rule that continues to this day to empower its employees to delight customers. According to the rule, every employee is allowed to spend up to $2,000 to use their judgment to rescue the guest experience without having to ask any manager.

This enables employees to take ownership, quick action when necessary, and feel a sense of pride and commitment, resulting in exceptional service that distinguishes them from their competitors.

Another great example is Southwest Airlines, which has long been a poster child for creating a great culture and has found leading with context, not control, is the way to go.

Even in a highly regulated industry like theirs, they have found ways to give their flight attendants freedom within a framework. For example, when it comes to communicating the routine FAA message for each flight, they provide flight attendants with the absolute critical statements that must be communicated but give them creative license in how they deliver it.

If you've ever experienced one of their flight attendants applying their unique flavor by rapping or singing the message, it's quite entertaining. This is just one example that exemplifies how granting your employees greater autonomy fosters engagement and innovation that differentiates your organization and products.

Providing increased agency also scales leadership across the organization. A great way to do this is to push decision rights as low in the organization as possible to increase agility, speed, ownership, and satisfaction.

FedEx did this, even in the early days when the company was struggling to survive. There is a famous story about a customer who needed her wedding dress sent from the East to the West Coast overnight. As the story goes, no other company could guarantee it would arrive in time, and FedEx didn't even have a plane scheduled to make that route.

However, the founder, Fred Smith, had always assured his employees that each team member possessed the authority to make decisions that aligned with the best interests of FedEx and its customers. So, one FedEx employee took this seriously and chartered a private plane to deliver the dress overnight.

Not only did it arrive in time for the wedding, but it turns out this woman was the daughter of Eastman Kodak's founder. She was so elated that she couldn't stop talking about it to all her guests at the wedding. Many of these guests were leaders of Fortune 500 companies, and the rest is history.

That decision was certainly a risk, but because Smith empowered employees to make decisions and it was implicit in the culture to take ownership and solve problems, everyone did it, without managing their status or worrying about getting approval.

In addition to an environment where people have the autonomy and agency to take action, employees need access to information and strategy to make smart decisions.

Transparency

Transparency, while always a cornerstone of a good culture, becomes increasingly important in a fast-moving, high-agency environment. When leaders share information freely with their employees, it not only reduces anxiety and democratizes context, but also helps cultivate a deeper understanding of the business and its operations.

Think about it—if employees don't know the business strategy or where the organization is trying to go, how can they help the organization get there? However, armed with this information, employees can act like owners and make better decisions that contribute to the company's success.

Netflix is a great example of this, having built a culture of transparency and treating people like adults, giving them the freedom and trust to make their own decisions. According to founder Reed Hastings, this approach has led to increased collaboration, efficiency, fairness, speed, innovation, and inclusion.

The effects of this can even be seen on a chemical level. Dr. Paul Zak's research shows when people have the autonomy to do something their way, it even frees up cognitive resources to find shortcuts and innovate.

I'm often asked by leaders whether it's risky to share too much with employees—whether transparency about challenges, financials, or strategic uncertainties might create panic or a loss of confidence. In my experience, the opposite is true.

Employees are perceptive. They already sense when the business is under pressure, when leadership is uncertain, when the strategy is changing. The question is not whether they will know—it's whether they'll hear it from you, in context, with a plan, or piece it together themselves from fragments and social media. The former builds trust; the latter destroys it.

Providing transparency and the ability to take action is just one side of the coin. Equally important is recognizing and appreciating employees' contributions.

Unfortunately, many employees feel undervalued and unappreciated at work. Gallup recently found only 40% of employees feel they received recognition for their work.

Research shows that when employees feel unrecognized, or a manager takes credit for their work, it registers in the brain to be as traumatic as a physical assault. A recent study by Deloitte found that the biggest contributor to burnout was a lack of recognition from leadership.

Lack of acknowledgment and appreciation is a morale killer and a major reason why so many people left their jobs during the Great Resignation. But recognizing employees doesn't have to be difficult or expensive.

Recognition and Rewards

Implementing a recognition program can have a huge impact on the bottom line. Companies with a program like this have 31% less voluntary turnover. Employees who feel valued are motivated to give their best at work.

Research by Gallup and Workhuman shows that putting employee recognition at the center of your workplace can quadruple employee engagement and save the organization, on average, $2.4 million annually. Recognition reinforces high performance because it highlights what good looks like, and what's rewarded gets repeated.

There are many ways to recognize employees beyond promotions and bonuses. Simply giving someone praise lights up the brain in the same way as getting a financial bonus.

At the organizational level, you can incorporate recognition into your culture and ways of working. Digital platforms like Kudoboard, Workhuman, and Slack channels are great ways to scale recognition.

Sharing success stories and recognizing employees for going above and beyond for customers during town halls, on the company website, and in social media posts will win your employees' and customers' hearts and minds.

It's key that the recognition is authentic, commensurate with the work done, and distributed in real time, as often as possible—Gallup suggests at least once a week.

Appreciation shouldn't be limited to an annual awards ceremony or performance review, but rather woven into the fabric of daily interactions.

You can start this with a simple yet powerful technique called purposeful affirmation. It begins with recalling the specific situation in which someone made a difference for you and identifying and naming their unique strengths and behaviors contributing to that impact. Most importantly, it's about showing them the profound effect they had on you or someone else.

Bonus points if you make recognition peer-to-peer. Peers have the biggest influence on employee engagement levels, and in this, appreciation benefits both the receiver and the giver. Social recognition gives employees at all levels a voice while providing an opportunity to demonstrate shared values.

I had a client who created a peer-nominated awards program for people who exemplified the organization's values. They held monthly award ceremonies where people would award each other in front of the organization. Practices like these have a ripple effect of fostering trust and strengthening bonds among colleagues.

Progressive organizations are taking the concepts of agency, accountability, and appreciation to new heights by adopting shared ownership models. These models empower employees with genuine ownership over their work and the outcomes it produces.

While shared ownership models have been around for some time, they remain surprisingly uncommon, despite their proven ability to enhance company culture, boost employee engagement, improve retention rates, foster inclusion, and ultimately drive profits.

Witnessing the compelling results firsthand, Pete Stavros, co-head of Americas Private Equity at the investment firm KKR, took the initiative to establish Ownership Works, a nonprofit organization dedicated to implementing employee ownership models across its portfolio of companies.

What sets Ownership Works apart is its comprehensive approach. They not only provide employees with shared equity arrangements but also undertake a holistic transformation of the organizational culture. This includes actively listening to employee feedback, responding to their concerns, and integrating their input into the company's operations.

Additionally, Ownership Works offers financial education and coaching to employees, equipping them with the knowledge and skills to effectively manage their newfound equity. By combining these elements, Ownership Works drives positive change and fosters a sense of ownership among employees, benefiting both individuals and the overall organization.

A great example of this is KKR's sale of C.H.I. Overhead Doors. Through its ownership program, all eight hundred employees—ranging from factory workers and truck drivers to senior managers—were provided with an equity payout averaging $175,000.

This initiative not only instilled a sense of pride, gratitude, and transformative financial benefits for the employees but also fostered an ownership mindset among them. And the business saw a 4x increase in EBITDA and revenue growth of 750%.

When employees are respected, recognized, and given the authority to make decisions, they develop a natural bias for action and the confidence to stretch and expand their capabilities. This is critical to grow them as a professional and drive the business forward in new ways.

Chapter 12

Make Them a Better Version of Themselves

One of our most essential human needs is to feel like we are leveraging our strengths, growing, and achieving our potential. Yet only 5% of people feel like they are meeting their full potential at work.

Contrary to the old model of going to school, getting a job, and plateauing into the status quo over the course of one's career, today we are living longer, with longer careers, and the environment necessitates the need for continuous upskilling, learning, and unlearning throughout.

Millennials and Gen Z are acutely aware of this and want to ensure the time they spend with your organization isn't a waste.

Microsoft found 76% of people would stay at their organization longer if they had more opportunities for learning and growth, yet 55% believe changing companies is the best way to develop their skills.

Millennial and Gen Z employees, in particular, crave growth and development and relentlessly desire progress. The minute they begin to feel stagnant, they are willing to walk.

There is a big opportunity here for organizations to provide work that leverages the skills, experience, and passions of their people while growing them into better versions of themselves. These opportunities are inexpensive, intrinsically motivating, and directly contribute to business outcomes simultaneously.

While Chapter 8 highlights several ways to develop and support managers specifically, here, let's talk about ways you can increase the engagement and performance of all your people by activating potential and mastery.

Leveraging Strengths

Helping your employees leverage their strengths activates what London Business School professor Dan Cable calls the seeking system, or the ventral striatum. This increases intrinsic motivation, enjoyment, and performance.

He suggests starting with the practice of creating a personal "highlight reel" as part of an onboarding exercise.

This involves having the employee reach out to a few people in their personal and professional network and asking them to share an anecdote of when the person made an impact or was being the best version of themselves.

After collecting the memories, the employee has a personal "highlight reel" to refer back to. But don't stop there—as Professor Cable advises, the next step is to turn those strengths into habits.

By job crafting and intentionally seeking out new activities that play to their strengths, employees can tap into their full potential and continue to grow and develop.

Personal Purpose

One of the most valuable and high-impact activities you can offer is to help your people discern and actualize their purpose. In Chapter 6, we discussed the organization's purpose. Here we will dive into helping employees discern their personal purpose.

McKinsey research shows that people who feel they can live their purpose at work have four times higher engagement and five times higher well-being. The study found people who don't feel they can live their purpose at work have lower energy, engagement, and life satisfaction.

The study also found frontline employees are ten times less likely to have opportunities to reflect on their purpose at work than those in leadership positions. There is a big opportunity for organizations to close this gap at zero cost.

There are many practical ways to help employees uncover their purpose, including holding workshops and providing digital courses that enable people to reflect.

One powerful tool is the Japanese concept of Ikigai, which involves reflecting on four key areas: what you love, what you're good at, what you can be paid for, and what the world needs. By finding the overlap between these four elements, individuals can uncover their unique purpose and bring greater meaning to their work and life.

Another approach is to engage in a values determination exercise, such as the one developed by Dr. John Demartini. His exercise helps individuals identify their top values and determine how to live in alignment with them.

Other reflection questions can include: "What is something you know to be true that no one told you?" "What problem in the world makes you angry or breaks your heart?" "What activities would you do even if you weren't being paid?" "What do others say you're good at or should do more of?" "If you had all the money in the world, how would you spend your time?"

Aligning Purposes

Bonus points if you can connect your employees' individual purpose with the broader organizational purpose.

Several years ago, Unilever started offering a leadership development program in which several hundred senior leaders uncovered their purpose and were able to connect that purpose to Unilever's purpose of "making sustainable living commonplace." Leaders were then able to use it to guide their work.

After seeing how impactful the program was, they expanded it to all levels of the organization. Today, over 29% of their global workforce has attended the one-day workshop. It has become such a core pillar of the culture that, often, people introduce themselves by sharing their purpose.

In the workshop, employees develop individualized plans that chart their desired path over the next eighteen months, personally and professionally, as well as the skills they will need to develop to get there.

These workshops, coupled with frequent check-ins, have been shown to increase engagement, well-being, and commitment to driving the company's strategy.

In 2019, 83% of those who had attended the workshop reported being inspired to go the extra mile, compared with only 53% of those who had not attended one.

Intentional Work Design

Organizations that view their employees within the constraints of the bullets in a job description are limiting their potential and forcing them to play small.

The result? The organization loses out on creativity, innovation, and employees' desire to go above and beyond, ultimately leading to high turnover rates.

It's no wonder the workforce is seeking opportunities outside of their day job that allow them to apply their skills, explore their interests, and continue to grow.

But here's the thing: there are plenty of ways that organizations can leverage their employees' strengths and desire for growth to achieve their business goals.

In his book *Love + Work*, Marcus Buckingham reveals doing work we love has the same effect on our brain as falling in love with someone. It releases a chemical cocktail of oxytocin, dopamine, and norepinephrine that provides a source of energy and resilience.

These neurotransmitters lead to faster and better cognitive performance, optimism, loyalty, productivity, resilience to stress, and higher retention rates. So why wouldn't you intentionally design the work to allow your employees to tap into their passions, strengths, and high performance?

Job Crafting

Yale and Wharton professor Amy Wrzesniewski's seminal work around job crafting has demonstrated how minor tweaks can transform a mundane job into a fulfilling and meaningful experience. This can include changes in responsibilities, tasks, or who employees interact with.

I had the opportunity to put this into practice a few years ago while leading a new team. I worked with my team to personalize their roles so that they could be most successful.

In my first one-on-one with each person, I asked them about their goals, interests, and what they enjoyed most about their work. I also asked what they would change about their jobs if they had the chance.

I discovered some team members were not utilizing their strengths to the fullest, while others were bored due to over-indexing on theirs. And some simply wanted to try something new.

So, together we matched the skills, experience, and preferred areas of growth of each team member with the needs of the business, and as a result, productivity, motivation, and engagement soared.

Upskilling

Providing opportunities for your employees to learn new skills not only increases their effectiveness in your business but also expands their capacity to take on more challenging tasks. And let's not forget the fact that it makes the work more interesting for them.

One of my clients recently launched a digital upskilling program and has seen excellent results. Through capability academies, employees can learn how to master Tableau, Alteryx, and AI skills, and even create bots to accomplish certain tasks.

The most innovative ideas have even contributed to new product offerings. Upskilling your workforce not only benefits your organization but is one of the top employee value propositions you can offer your people.

Internal Marketplaces

Mastercard has taken a people-centric approach to talent management with the launch of its internal talent marketplace powered by Gloat. The platform provides employees with democratized access to opportunities for developing their careers.

By redeploying people where their skills were needed internally, Mastercard avoided laying off any employees during the pandemic. Their internal marketplace also saves them from outsourcing projects to contractors. With the platform's ability to connect employees across geographies and business units, it also fosters collaboration and breaks down silos within the organization.

Apprenticeship Programs

Apprenticeship programs are a powerful tool for developing and engaging your workforce while boosting your business's productivity.

A few years ago I led a learning and development team that created an apprentice program to enable employees from other teams to dedicate a portion of their time to upskilling, shadowing, and working on real projects.

This provided a way for people from other departments to build relationships and learn new skills while adding bandwidth to the team, and as a result, we didn't need to hire additional employees for those projects.

Reverse Mentoring

Several years ago, one of my clients was transitioning from Lotus Notes to Gmail and other Google collaboration tools. Most of the senior people in the company were Native Analogs—not comfortable with the new technology and ways of working. So we created a reverse mentoring program that partnered leaders with a more junior Digital Native consultant.

This model created a triple benefit of white-glove-level knowledge transfer to the more senior people while building professional confidence and cultivating leadership skills in the junior staff.

As a bonus, because people are matched randomly, the reverse and cross-mentoring model can also mitigate the unconscious bias that can happen when senior leaders choose who they mentor organically. Having a specific topic to guide the mentoring relationship adds structure and accountability to ensure everyone benefits from the program.

Learning in the Flow of Work

The conventional practice of transporting employees to a conference room and subjecting them to three days of lectures from an instructor is not only costly but also ineffective.

This is particularly true for today's workforce, who prefer to learn from bite-sized, on-demand content.

Learning in the flow of work is a significantly more productive, cost-effective, and engaging approach. Real-time coaching and feedback from managers, mentors, peers, and digital adoption platforms such as WalkMe enable the immediate application of knowledge to the tasks at hand.

Embrace Side Hustles

While a key motivator for human beings is seeing progress and meaningful output of their efforts, most jobs don't do a good job of demonstrating this.

A 2023 study by Zapier found over a third of employees have side hustles in addition to their full-time jobs, and that number is only growing.

Embracing the reality that many of your employees are engaged in side hustles can unlock a significant source of motivation that might otherwise be overlooked while attempting to prevent it.

Side hustles offer increased outlets for cultivating their network, creativity, and skills in a low-risk environment, which can help fill the void left by a day job.

Companies need to understand that the beauty of intrinsic motivation is that it's not finite. Finding energy, inspiration, and motivation outside of work spills over and motivates all areas of people's lives, including their day jobs.

Side hustles often provide upskilling the organization doesn't have to pay for, and your employees bring those skills back into their roles.

As long as your people are meeting the expectations of their day job, don't worry about their outside endeavors.

I recently worked with a consulting firm that not only encouraged employee side hustles but created an incubator where partners and employees were able to become early investors in the ideas, and many even formed new lines of business for the firm.

Peer Coaching

While mentoring is a powerful way to transfer knowledge from someone who has the expertise to someone who wants to learn, peer coaching is more about working with a colleague to validate and activate knowledge about oneself.

The coaching approach enables participants to engage in social learning, without the need for screening for specific knowledge or experience.

It also avoids reinforcing hierarchy and dependence on senior employees.

Exploration

Dopamine is central to motivation, but the mechanism matters. It's released through the brain's seeking system; the ventral striatum, which activates when we pursue something uncertain but potentially rewarding. It's about the anticipatory drive toward it.

This is why environments that invite employees to explore, learn, and experiment tend to produce more sustained engagement than those structured around performance targets alone.

The seeking itself is the reward signal — which means intrinsic motivation and performance follow naturally, rather than needing to be separately engineered.

Google was a perfect example of the power of the seeking system when it implemented its 20% rule, which allowed employees to spend a day per week working on creative projects of their choice.

These projects have produced innovative products like Google Maps and Gmail. Putting this into effect can be as simple as giving your team a half day once a week or once a month for personal development.

To ensure accountability, some organizations ask for quarterly presentations where each team member presents a short overview of what they explored, learned, and the implications of their work.

By providing opportunities for your employees to explore, you not only increase their performance and motivation but also create a culture of innovation and creativity within your organization.

Netflix Your LMS

Gone are the days of relying solely on traditional training methods to upskill your workforce.

With access to Google, YouTube, and TikTok, today's workforce can quickly learn anything they need to know on the fly.

Organizations today must provide a modern, dynamic learning management system (LMS) that operates like Netflix, pushing personalized, bite-sized articles, podcasts, and videos to employees based on factors such as role, tenure, team, interests, and previous searches in the learning catalog.

Some of the more effective platforms also assign tasks such as connecting with a person on a certain team about a certain topic.

Platforms like Obrizum deliver personalized and adaptive learning, leveraging AI and machine learning, as well as analytics to inform team building, workforce management, and career progression.

Investing in and developing your employees enables them to become better, more actualized versions of themselves.

This not only increases their motivation, engagement, and performance but makes them more valuable to your organization and customers.

Here's the bottom line: the organizations that invest most deeply in developing their people don't lose them faster—they keep them longer.

The research consistently shows that employees who feel genuinely developed and supported are more engaged, more loyal, and more productive.

And when they do eventually leave, they leave as ambassadors—referrers, clients, partners, and boomerang hires.

The return on development investment compounds over time in ways that are hard to fully capture on a balance sheet.

Any leader who has watched a team of curious, growing, challenged people perform at an extraordinary level knows exactly what it feels like.

Chapter 13

The Art of Meaning Making

Whereas having purpose is about *why* you do what you do, meaning is the feeling that you have an impact beyond yourself.

Studies show that when we help another person, or even think about our impact on others, it provides a boost of the "happiness trifecta" of oxytocin, dopamine, and serotonin.

Meaning comes from satisfying our human need for transcendence, our innate desire to go beyond our self-interests and view the world from a wider perspective.

It's the urge to make an impact, solve complex problems, and contribute, and gives us the feeling that our existence holds significance.

Yet, in today's world, many of us struggle to find a sense of coherence and meaning in our daily lives.

This is especially true for Millennials and Gen Z, who are experiencing a heightened sense of anxiety and existential dread as they search for meaning in a world that feels increasingly fragmented and disconnected.

One major contributor to this phenomenon is that traditional sources of meaning, such as religion, community, and familial rituals, are no longer as prevalent or accessible as they once were.

Additionally, the type of work that most of us engage in today is often abstract, complex, and removed from the tangible impact it has on others.

As a result, many people feel disconnected and unfulfilled in their jobs, which can lead to a sense of existential emptiness that permeates every aspect of their lives.

Meaning matters. It is not merely a superficial or feel-good notion—instead, it possesses the power to exponentially propel individuals forward and is a critical component of employee engagement, productivity, innovation, and overall well-being.

The benefits of meaningful work extend far beyond the workplace. Studies have shown that individuals who find purpose in their jobs are less likely to experience heart attacks, stroke, and burnout.

The importance of meaningful work is so significant that a recent BetterUp study found over 90% of people would be willing to take a pay cut—up to 23% of their total lifetime earnings—if it meant having a more fulfilling and meaningful job.

And for Millennials and Gen Z, the impact of meaningful work on retention is even more pronounced. According to a Great Place to Work study, people are three times more likely to stay in a job if they believe it has meaning.

So, how can companies inspire their employees to experience this seemingly elusive feeling about their work? Your organization doesn't need to be curing cancer or saving the planet to make the work meaningful. It's all about how people think about the work they are doing and whether they can see how it impacts others.

Ways to Build Meaning Into Work

Create Mattering

The need to feel connected and as if we matter is so crucial to our well-being that the US Surgeon General recently named it a top priority for improving mental health in the workplace.

Despite this, 50% of employees today feel unseen, invisible, and undervalued in their jobs. If your organization struggles with issues around motivation, disengagement, or retention, a lack of mattering is likely at the root of the problem.

Mattering is a key precursor to employee engagement. Without that feeling, individuals are unlikely to feel invested or committed to their work.

But what does mattering mean in the context of the workplace? According to author and meaningful work researcher Zach Mercurio, PhD, mattering means feeling noticed, affirmed, and needed.

While belonging, and feeling welcome in a group are important, mattering takes that a step further by emphasizing the critical role that each individual plays in the success of the team or company as a whole.

When individuals feel like they truly matter—like their contributions are valued and recognized—they're more likely to be engaged, motivated, and productive in their work.

Show Their Role in the Bigger Picture

Tapping into the power of transcendence can be the key to unlocking an ethereal, yet priceless source of motivation and meaning.

By fostering a culture that encourages employees to transcend their individual goals and connect with a larger purpose, organizations can achieve their business objectives while creating a more fulfilling work environment.

It all comes down to connecting the dots and positioning the work in a deliberate way that gives people a clear understanding of how their role makes a difference to others. This makes them feel part of something truly special.

When they understand why what they're doing matters, work transforms from completing tasks and hitting targets into a purposeful mission.

A job becomes a calling that inspires them to be their best selves and make a real difference.

Highlight Interdependence

Organizations often make the mistake of throwing a group of highly intelligent individuals into a project without providing them with context and necessary role clarity. The result is confusion, redundant work, frustration, and burnout.

However, when leaders are intentional about outlining clear roles and responsibilities based on each team member's unique strengths and interests—and showing how each person's work impacts the whole—it can create magic.

There are several powerful tools to leverage in cultivating interdependence. One of my favorites is leveraging storytelling to highlight the impact that each person has on the team. Storytelling can also show the impact the team has on the broader organization and community.

One of my clients includes questions in performance reviews that ask how a person's work has impacted or benefited others. Another tactic I've seen clients leverage is a central platform where teams can update the organization on their work and share ways others can help. This allows people across the organization to see how everything connects.

It's also important to reward teams as a whole, rather than just individual star performers, to foster a sense of community and shared success.

Creating a Shared Purpose to Rally the Team

Establishing a shared identity that aligns with the goal helps employees see that even the most trivial parts of their job are integral to the team's and/or organization's success.

Take, for example, the way NASA enabled thousands of employees with very different roles to rally around the common goal of a lunar landing.

There is a famous interaction between John F. Kennedy and a NASA janitor at the space center. Kennedy asked him, "What do you do here, and why are you working so late?" The janitor replied, "I'm helping put a man on the moon."

Wharton School researcher Andrew Carton found that one way NASA made people in every role feel connected to that big purpose was through the actions leaders took to build a strong connection between employees' daily responsibilities and NASA's ultimate aspirations.

The first thing leaders did was narrow the focus to one objective and reframe the abstract objective of "advancing science by exploring the solar system" to become the more specific "put a man on the moon." As Carton states, reframing lofty, abstract organizational goals as a more concrete objective and helping employees connect their day-to-day work to the objective is essential.

One of the ways they operationalized this idea was the Ladder to the Moon, which leaders scrawled on blackboards in NASA facilities.

At the bottom of the ladder were the group's tasks. The next rung up was a tangible, measurable objective that the tasks made possible. The next rung was the concrete, quantifiable goal that the former objective made possible, and so on until the top rung: "To put a person on the moon by the end of the decade to advance science." This helped people see how their work contributed to NASA's big, audacious goal.

Show the Impact of Their Work

A few years ago, Adam Grant conducted a study that revealed how getting employees closer to the customer improved bottom-line outcomes. He separated university alumni call center employees into 3 groups who spent 5 minutes before work reading stories.

The group who read stories from alumni who had been able to attend the university thanks to the money raised by the call center in the past brought in more than double the number of donations they had before the exercise, far outperforming either of the other 2 groups.

Leaders can get people closer to the end product of their work by collecting and sharing stories across the organization, the website, and social media, highlighting how employees work with their clients and colleagues.

Sharing what employees liked most about their clients, what problem or pain point they solved, and how their contributions directly impact the customer, the community, and/or the broader world, helps employees see the significance and necessity of their work.

A fantastic example of this in action is the study done by Harvard professor Ryan Buell with restaurant chefs. He simply set up an iPad with an open videoconference in the dining area and the kitchen.

Because the chefs could now see the customers, it made the chefs feel like what they did mattered. This increased customer satisfaction by 10% and the chefs reported feeling more appreciated, more satisfied with their jobs, and more willing to exert effort.

Intentional Language

Developing simple, compelling taglines that convey to employees that they are part of a larger mission or solving a bigger problem can be powerful as well.

For example, I once met the CEO of a large paint brand who would often say to his people, "There's no more affordable way to transform somebody's home than a fresh can of paint." This reminded his employees they were part of the larger mission to help customers do more with less to make a positive impact on their lives.

Sensemaking

When organizations approach work and projects through a process-oriented perspective, they often overlook the employee experience of it, leading to a loss of intrinsic meaning. This is an easy fix.

Leaders should be communicating at the beginning, throughout, and at the end of the project how each person made a difference and their impact on the project. This is especially important if the project is stopped partway through or if people get switched off the project prior to completion.

It's important to show people how the hours they spent mattered on some level. Even if it didn't go to market or have an amazing result, they need to feel that all of it was worth it, because someone noticed and recognized it.

The organizations that get meaning right are those that make it a continuous practice, not a one-time communication. They build it into the rhythms of work: the way they open team meetings, the questions they ask in performance reviews, the stories they tell in town halls, the way they close out projects.

Over time, these small acts compound into a culture where people feel, at a fundamental level, that what they do matters.

And when that's true—when the work feels like it has genuine significance—the discretionary effort, the innovation, the loyalty, and the retention follow naturally.

You can't mandate meaning. But you can create the conditions for it to emerge.

Now that we've looked at various ways organizations can meet employees' human needs, let's talk about how to design a transformative, end-to-end employee experience that incorporates these principles.

Chapter 14

Your Company IS the Product: The EX Delivers the CX

Organizations are starting to see that employee experience (EX) is the key driver of customer experience (CX) and are finding new ways to connect the two.

The experience your frontline employees have every day is the model for how they deliver your brand. For example, a company cannot expect to deliver a cutting-edge, seamless, and intuitive customer experience if its internal processes are slow, bureaucratic, and friction-filled for employees.

Similarly, if your company does not promote and ensure the employee experience demonstrates empathy, service, and personalization, it is unlikely that your employees will deliver those qualities in their service to customers.

A great example of this is Amazon, which is known for being customer-centric at the expense of its people. After losing a quarter of its profit—eight billion dollars—to employee turnover of around 150% in 2021, they are now looking at becoming the "best place to work on the planet."

Employee experience is not about employee "happiness" programs, foosball tables, or Taco Tuesdays.

These are cosmetic things that may give you a slight, short-term bump in engagement, but the sustainable motivation, productivity, and discretionary effort you strive for come from the ongoing experience.

Organizations that focus on the end-to-end experience, including all of the touchpoints between employees and the organization, see significant benefits.

Research from MIT and human resources thought leader Josh Bersin found that a great employee experience produces three times more innovation, creates change agility in the organization, increases engagement five times over, improves retention and belonging of their people, and doubles customer satisfaction and revenue conversion.

However, organizations must be as deliberate about designing, nurturing, and monitoring it as they do the customer experience to produce these benefits.

In her book *The Experience Mindset*, Tiffani Bova, Salesforce Innovation Evangelist, highlights research that shows companies who get EX and CX right yield a 9.7x greater growth rate than those who don't. She says, "The fastest way to get customers to love your brand is to get employees to love their job."

What the EX Entails

Spanning culture, technology, physical space, and the employee life cycle, the EX starts the moment a candidate has first heard of your organization—when they think about your brand in the marketplace—to when they start looking at you on Glassdoor, to interviewing, to the onboarding experience, the way you grow and develop them, to how you offboard them, how you interact with them as an alum, and all the "moments that matter" in between.

Like your customer experience, it's every minute people are engaged with your organization and how it makes them feel.

Think about it as strategically designing the time people spend with your company in a way that creates value for them so that they can create value for your customers.

A critical component of a great employee experience is the removal of sources of friction—or any ways the organization makes employees feel stifled, unwelcome, or like they are simply valued to be extracted.

Let's take a look at friction, how it impacts the employee experience, and how you can remove it.

From Friction to Flow

Never has anyone said they love the soul-sucking friction they have to deal with at work. Yet, it continues to be one of the most expensive and exhausting attributes of our work experience.

If we look at the top causes of the Great Resignation, quiet quitting, and other forms of disengagement, they all fall into the category of friction.

Friction is the cumulative effect of clunky technology, needless meetings, excessive communications, bureaucratic processes, lack of transparency, and emotionally exhausting interactions.

Friction is the second shift employees have to work, on top of their day job, which—by the way—they don't get paid or promoted for. It's depleting their time and energy, sucking their souls, and costing organizations well over $1 trillion annually.

Today's workforce is particularly allergic to it because they've grown up in a world designed to be as friction-free as possible.

Think of your organization as a product for your people. Is it easy to use? Are there "bugs"? How does it make them feel? Is it relevant? What do they get out of it? What are the barriers?

Asking questions like this can help you streamline, automate, and kill off your friction darlings so people can focus on the real work. Which of the following flavors of friction is your organization most guilty of?

Outdated, Clunky, Disparate Tools and Tech

In our hyper-personalized, easy-to-use, on-demand world of AI, Amazon, Netflix, and Apple, why does it feel like 1985 inside our organizations?

Modern technology is key to attracting and retaining Millennials and Gen Z employees—73% said they would leave an organization if the technology was terrible.

Remember, they haven't had the experience of older generations who gradually moved from primitive tools to what's available now. We can't blame them for being frustrated when they have to step back in time to go to work.

To create a more Millennial and Gen-Z friendly tech environment, ask yourself: Does your organization use disparate platforms that don't talk to each other? How can you integrate them more seamlessly, utilizing single sign-on and artificial intelligence to minimize entering redundant information? Default to giving employees more access to technology and tools, not less.

Processes That Should Be Automated and Digitized

Ask how much clutter or extra work your company requires employees to engage in to get things done. Are there excessive hierarchies, miles of approvals, and analysis paralysis when making decisions?

To enhance speed and agility within the organization, consider implementing guardrails or guiding principles that empower lower levels of the organization to make decisions autonomously. Have you leveraged technology to automate the mundane and elevate the strategic, more humane work?

This is especially important for managers. Now, more than ever, they are being asked to play a more strategic, empathic, and connective role with their people. They can't do that if buried in robotic, low-value administrative tasks.

Lack of Prioritization

If everything is a priority, nothing is. Avoid the "flavor of the month" inertia that often comes with each new initiative, by ruthlessly prioritizing and clearly communicating the top strategic priorities the organization is focused on.

This makes it easy for people to focus and say no to anything that doesn't directly ladder up to those priorities. It's also critical to make it evident to employees how all the initiatives and programs fit together, why they are important, who they impact, and the benefits.

Operating Reactively

Focus on the signal, not the noise. We've all seen departments like HR operating as order-takers, putting out fires, and building bolt-on programs to address business problems reactively. This gives them a bad name and creates wasteful, unimpactful work.

However, magic happens when these teams work proactively with the business to understand and address the root causes of their pain points. The strategy of each function—Finance, HR, IT—should operationalize the overall business strategy by being grounded in solving the business issues.

Meetings. PERIOD

Stop making meetings the default. A recent study reported that organizations spend roughly 23% of their time on meetings, with 71% of them considered unproductive. This costs an estimated $1.4 billion annually.

Ask yourself: are your meetings short, strategic, and few? Or are people in meetings all day, unable to get work done until after hours?

The Canadian e-commerce company Shopify recently led the way in a calendar purge, eliminating recurring meetings and freeing up 32,400 hours yearly for other work. They have even gone as far as to roll out a calculator embedded in their calendar app that estimates the cost of any meeting with three or more people.

A great way to vet whether you need a meeting and ensure you're getting the optimal impact from it is Keith Ferrazzi's practice of having the meeting leader share a Google doc with the proposed attendees before the meeting and let them weigh in on the topic(s).

From there, the leader decides whether a meeting is needed from the feedback. Often it is not. If it is needed, determine the minimal number of most relevant people needed in the meeting. Then, the meeting is much more streamlined and strategically focused on making a decision.

Failing to Leverage Data Strategically

One of the biggest mistakes I see is organizations not leveraging the enormous amount of data available to them to inform decisions, programs, and ways of working.

Make it a priority to ensure clean, integrated, and connected data across your organization. This improves decision-making, enables more strategic operations, and improves the employee experience by minimizing redundant work and increasing personalization.

Lack of Clarity

Today's workforce was raised in a very structured and organized way—they are used to transparency, crystal-clear expectations, and even checklists.

When they walk into your organization, they are looking for the same explicit expectations, goals, and metrics that spell out exactly what they need to do to be successful.

Creating this sense of certainty is key to reducing what neuroscience calls a threat response, which derails focus, motivation, and effectiveness.

Managers and leaders can do this by making clear what the expectations are and what outcomes would be desirable.

Team agreements are useful tools for providing transparency around what the team needs to show up as their best selves. These often lay out channels, boundaries, availability, and other expectations for working well together.

Not Connecting the Dots

Ensure people have the context to see how everything fits together. This means noting how each project, platform, program, etc., ladders to the organizational strategy and how it connects to other departments, teams, programs, and the customer.

This enables people to see the organization as a system of connected pieces and a cohesive narrative instead of disparate and random.

Lack of Transparency

In today's world, everyone is a broadcaster and if you don't provide your people with info and updates as quickly as possible, they'll see it on social media, which will erode trust faster than you can send a tweet.

Leaders are criticized 9 times more for under, than over-communicating. Sharing freely with your people democratizes context and reduces the anxiety experienced in the absence of information.

Push information as far down the organization as possible — open up departmental meetings, Slack channels, and documents to everyone. When people at every level have access to the full picture, better decisions get made faster, and ideas emerge from unexpected places.

Ineffective Communication

Everyone's overbooked, burned out, and overwhelmed. To break through, be more targeted and brief. Do the up-front work to understand what your audience needs to know, why they should care, and what they need to do.

Structure communications to save recipients from decoding a brain dump and ask yourself if it even needs to be an email. Email overload costs $1,800 per employee annually. Could it be a Slack message, voice memo, or one-on-one agenda item instead?

Borrow from the pros: Joseph Campbell's Hero's Journey — the framework behind Star Wars, TED Talks, and Airbnb — is your model. Cast the employee as the hero, and the leader as the guide calling them to action.

Micromanagement

Managers, stop over-functioning! Even unintentional micromanagement causes resentment, burnout, robs employees of development, and sucks the meaning out of work.

It also mitigates accountability because if the manager is always there to cover it, people don't feel the need to take ownership. Even the highest performers will suffer from learned helplessness in this environment.

The time and energy the micromanager wastes delving into the weeds should be reallocated to managing up or managing the client.

Nail the "Moments That Matter"

In Unreasonable Hospitality, restaurateur Will Guidara reveals the art of creating small but profound moments for people. A mentee of Danny Meyer, Guidara shares how he once rushed out to buy a New York City hot dog for a guest at Michelin-starred 11 Madison Park — after overhearing them mention it was the one thing they'd missed on their trip. The guest retold the story endlessly.

Guidara also found that empowering employees to create these moments for customers naturally spilled over into how they treated each other.

Now imagine applying that same spirit to your employees. The cost is negligible — the ripple effects could be transformative.

Attract

Unlike organizations that position themselves as the main attraction, a strong Employee Value Proposition (EVP) spotlights the candidate as the hero. It compellingly answers: Why work here? What do I get? How do you compare?

But it has to be true. Organizations can no longer accentuate the positives without authentically portraying the reality of working there. Misalignment drives turnover, and replacing an employee can cost up to twice their salary, while the revolving door erodes productivity, culture, and morale for everyone left behind.

If your website is full of buzzwords and glossy stock photos that promise a vocational fairy tale but the reality doesn't measure up, employees will see through it fast. No one likes to feel catfished.

Hire

Leading organizations leverage AI to automate as much as possible behind the scenes: matching jobs to candidates, interview coordination, assessment, and follow-up, while ensuring a personalized experience for each candidate.

They also ensure their culture and values are embedded throughout the hiring process and all correspondence to new hires, so it feels like the brand from day one.

It's also important to survey candidates (regardless of if they join you) to understand the hiring experience, if there are gaps, anything they would improve, and even ask for a Glassdoor rating.

Onboard

Within 24 hours of a signed offer, send new hires swag and a welcome note from their manager and mentor buddy to celebrate the moment. Follow up with any required paperwork, training materials, and orientation details before day one.

Kick off onboarding with interactive sessions that bring culture to life — think escape rooms or charity projects to spark real connections. Assign each new hire a buddy, mentor, or culture champion, and plug them into relevant ERGs and communities from the start.

Finally, onboarding interviews — short informational chats with members of each department — are a great way to help new hires map the organization and build relationships early.

Leverage Other Pivotal Moments

Several moments outside the employee life cycle hold immense significance throughout the employee journey—from the joy of childbirth to the heaviness of grief or illness, to the excitement of promotions and birthdays.

These moments shape people's lives and inevitably impact their work. Failing to acknowledge these moments can leave employees feeling overlooked, undervalued, and as if the relationship is solely transactional.

Be sure to recognize the holistic human experience of your people by honoring these moments.

Offboard

Offboarding is an overlooked opportunity to leave a lasting impression and lay the groundwork for an ongoing relationship. Companies with strong alumni programs earn Glassdoor ratings that are consistently 16% higher.

Leaders like Accenture and McKinsey have found that nurturing alumni communities drives real returns — from client referrals to rehires.

These programs stay connected through social media, events, and newsletters, while some organizations, like Booz Allen Hamilton, tap their alumni pool for project-based and short-term staffing needs.

Done well, offboarding transforms departing employees into lasting ambassadors and future collaborators.

Bring It All to Life

Now that you see how the touchpoints fit together, here's how to bring it to life through design thinking, data, and AI.

Start with empathy and user-centered design. View every program, process, technology, and interaction through the lens of how it will impact employees, make them feel, and address their needs.

Understand your people as distinct personas — mapping their needs, pain points, and values through surveys, interviews, focus groups, and analytics. Journey-map their touchpoints to uncover friction and moments that matter.

The most common mistake: designing the employee experience in a single boardroom session with a homogenous group of senior leaders whose daily reality looks nothing like a frontline employee, new hire, or working caregiver.

Go to the source — ride-alongs, shadowing, co-design workshops with employees at every level yield insights no survey can capture.

Ensure leaders are aligned, visibly role-modeling the values and behaviors you're trying to build.

Pair that with a comprehensive listening and actioning strategy. Employees aren't survey fatigued — they're tired of sharing ideas and never hearing what happened.

Follow up fast, share what's being acted on and what isn't, and why. Nasdaq responds to surveys on a two-week cadence, driving measurable gains in accountability and engagement.

For high turnover, dig into root causes. One retail client facing record attrition combined engagement data, exit interviews, and focus groups to identify pain points, then deployed Red-Yellow-Green teams to replicate top-performing stores and shore up struggling ones.

Deliberately architecting a great employee experience is the foundation for both a great customer experience — and managing change effectively.

Chapter 15

Sending an Email Isn't Change Management

There is a common misconception that humans don't like change. I would argue that's not entirely true. People love change when it comes to buying a new iPhone, getting into a new relationship, or landing a new job.

What they don't like is a being changed. The problem is not change; it's ambiguity, uncertainty, and thrusting change upon people—especially if they're not equipped with what they need to make the change.

Change is unsettling because it strips away control and thrusts people into uncertainty, yet still demands action from a place of limited information. That psychological discomfort is real, and for many, it triggers a fight-or-flight response.

Change management bridges that gap by providing a structured approach to moving individuals, teams, and organizations from where their current to the future state.

Done well, it dissolves uncertainty by providing clear details: the why behind the change, how decisions were made, what it means for people, what's expected of them, the timeline, and how they'll be supported. It also mitigates the loss of control by building in as much autonomy, choice, and co-creation as possible.

Yet over 70% of organizational change efforts fail — leaving tons of time, money, energy, and credibility on the table.

Why Most Organizations Fail at Managing Change

People Don't See the "Why"

When people can't see the purpose of the change or what's in it for them, they're much more likely to resist it.

Harvard professor Ellen Langer's research shows that simply telling people "why" you want them to do something turns off the amygdala, or the part of the brain that prevents people from making changes because they see the situation through a fight-or-flight lens.

When sharing the "why", go beyond the business case and benefits to the organization. Employees don't care about how much money it saves the company; they need to see how it personally benefits them.

To discern this, put yourself in the shoes of the people going through the change and ask what's in it for them specifically. For example, if the organization is transitioning to a new software platform, you'll want to highlight enhanced collaboration, automation of tedious tasks, and a more user-friendly interface.

Change Theater

When leadership activity creates the appearance of commitment without the substance of it, you don't have a change initiative — you have change theater. And organizations are full of experienced audiences who can spot the difference immediately.

Sending an email is not leadership. Visible, consistent role-modeling is. People don't adopt new behaviors because they received a well-crafted communication — they adopt them because they watched someone they respect do it first, and saw that it was safe. Without that signal from the top, buy-in doesn't erode slowly. It evaporates.

Not Co-Creating With People

In an era of worker agency, democratized information, and social engagement, change can no longer be done to people — it must be done with them.

Too often, those leading change exclude the very people it affects from the design and planning process. This is a costly mistake: people rarely champion what they had no hand in creating, and leaders don't have enough visibility into the daily realities of their teams to get it right alone.

The fix is straightforward. Gartner research shows that involving employees in the design and planning of change increases success rates by 30%.

Thinking "Go Live" Means We're Done

No, we're not done. Change is not an event—it's a process. Launching a change is when the real change begins.

Change management doesn't stop once you've launched. You need a robust sustainability plan, including ongoing enablement, communications, listening, and iterating based on feedback loops.

Not Thinking Beyond the Technology

Leaders are often excited about digitally transforming their organizations without thinking beyond the technology. Clients often say, "I thought we just give our employees a login, and they would use the platform."

Becoming digital or AI-enabled isn't something you do — it's something you become. The tech is the smallest part of the transformation. It demands new mindsets, new behaviors, and a fundamental rewiring of how work gets designed, decisions get made, and value gets created.

Developing personas and journey-mapping users help ensure you capture the full breadth of changes required.

Waiting to Communicate

When leaders withhold information — whether they lack the details or don't want to rock the boat — it backfires.

Silence creates a breeding ground for rumor and speculation, and when people's brains fill in the gaps, they almost always produce a threat response that fuels resistance.

The antidote is simple: communicate early and often, even if the message is just "we don't have more to share yet, but we will." That alone can defuse anxiety and make people feel included rather than sidelined.

Not Getting in Front of Resistance

First, it's important to know that a moderate amount of resistance is positive—a complete absence of it means you're not threatening the status quo enough.

People typically resist change for 3 reasons:

- They don't get why they need to change (meaning you haven't brought them along—lead with the "why" behind the change and how it benefits them)

- They don't get it (meaning you haven't shown them what's changing and how they'll need to adapt to it)

- They don't like you (meaning you haven't built the relationship with them or brought them in to co-create with you). This commonly shows up as unanticipated emotional resistance.

Often, various unexpected emotions surface as people undergo the change process.

For emotions to be accelerators rather than inhibitors, change leaders must anticipate and put conditions in place to address them.

This includes creating psychological safety and providing mechanisms for all voices to be heard, such as listening sessions and focus groups.

I recently had a high-profile client launch a new SaaS platform, yet no one was using it. It turned out that middle managers ran the show—even more than senior leaders—yet no one had engaged them in the design and implementation plan for this new platform.

So, we held several workshops walking the managers through the vision, the why, the impacts, the benefits to all stakeholders, and asking for their feedback.

I cannot tell you how many DMs I received from the different managers after the sessions, telling me how much they appreciated that we included them and asked for their feedback.

This produced a far better implementation plan, as well as a major commitment from the managers to help their people adopt the platform.

Command and Control Approaches

Gone are the days when mandates and top-down directives could drive organizational change. Today's employees are empowered and demand more autonomy in their work.

We've witnessed the fallout from leaders who demanded a return to the office five days a week post-pandemic, only to face backlash and backpedaling.

This approach doesn't just fail to drive compliance — it actively triggers psychological reactance. Reactance is a powerful force that kicks in the moment someone feels pressured or commanded, even if it's something they already intended to do. It ignites the inner rebel, turning neutral ground into resistance and goodwill into resentment.

Lead Change in Ways People Want to Follow

In today's dynamic landscape, where people are stretched thin and change is coming at unprecedented rates, traditional, top-down approaches no longer work.

The key to success lies in putting your workforce at the center of your change efforts. This involves harnessing the power of human nature, leveraging behavioral economics, and embracing innovative design thinking methods.

Remove Friction

A strategy often employed in the customer experience realm is proactively addressing friction and resistance.

In their book *The Human Element*, professors Nordgren and Schonthal highlight these sources of friction, including the degree of change, the level of effort, and the emotions involved:

Degree of Change: People distrust the unknown and default to the status quo — even when it isn't working. To overcome this, make the unfamiliar familiar through pilots, samples, or repeated exposure.

Small asks like testing a product or providing feedback, ease people into change without triggering resistance.

Level of Effort: People take the path of least resistance, so make new behaviors as easy as possible. Give them a clear road map of what, how, and when. Share stories of what good looks like, and embed new behaviors into existing ways of working.

Emotional Reactions: This is the most overlooked lever. As AI, digitization, and robotics reshape work, employees can feel replaceable and irrelevant — triggering insecurity and resistance. Lead with what's in it for them (shedding mundane tasks to focus on creative, strategic, high-impact work only they can do).

When roles are evolving, share upskilling plans early — so change feels like an invitation to grow, not a threat to survive.

And whatever the situation, be transparent about motives. People can handle difficult news far better than they can handle uncertainty and doubt.

Co-Creation

We're in a new era of employee participation, and that demands new ways of bringing people along.

A people-led approach works best: structured enough to serve the organization, but flexible enough to give each person ownership of their change journey.

It starts with a collective vision everyone is invited to help shape — one that fosters inclusion, community, and shared purpose.

Leaders play a critical role in articulating the why, setting direction, and providing the training, tools, and resources people need to navigate what's ahead. But then — step back.

Nothing is mandated. Employees choose their learning methods and decide how much to opt in. Ownership inspires willingness; people embrace change they helped create, not change that was handed to them.

PwC's Digital Lab is a masterclass in this approach. Facing the rise of automation and AI, the firm made one thing clear from the start: this wasn't about cutting headcount — it was about helping people thrive. That framing inspired enthusiastic opt-in.

From there, PwC let employees choose what to learn and how — whether that meant a twenty-minute podcast on machine learning or collaborating with colleagues to streamline client workflows.

Critically, the initiative was driven by business leaders, not just HR — signaling that experimentation and growth were organizational priorities, not checkbox exercises.

As employees saw tangible results, their excitement became contagious, pulling more colleagues in. When people have a hand in shaping the future, they show up for it.

Start a Movement

Activate change from within by starting a movement that resonates with employees and propels your business strategy into action.

Unlike top-down approaches that often result in messages getting lost in the cascade, a movement takes a grassroots approach, leveraging existing networks and teams.

Movements tap into peer-to-peer motivation and inspiration, reflecting what employees truly care about and mobilizing them to become active participants.

To create a successful movement, Stanford Business School professor Sarah Soule advises following three key steps:

- **Enlist an elite ally:** A key senior leader spearheading initiative lends credibility.

- **Frame the issue Clearly:** Articulate what the movement stands for and what it asks through a compelling vision that makes the benefits personally and unmistakably clear.

- **Connect to the broader culture:** Tie your movement to the broader business strategy or a larger issue relevant to the zeitgeist.

One of my favorite examples comes from a large media conglomerate navigating rapid industry disruption.

Rather than relying on top-down directives, the company tapped its most influential employees — dubbed Innovation Catalysts — to drive change from within.

Drawn from every department and level, these Catalysts were equipped with resources, training, and support to sharpen their skills as change agents.

Their mandate: spread a culture of collaboration and innovation through their networks, inspire new thinking, and lead by example.

They hosted innovation forums, presented case studies, ran workshops, and built an internal online hub where employees across departments and geographies could connect, share ideas, and collaborate.

Their influence rippled through the organization — breaking down silos, sparking cross-functional collaboration, and making innovation everyone's agenda, not just leadership's.

Leverage Behavioral Economics

The neo-behavioral approach to change operates under the radar by employing nudges, choice architecture, and environmental design to produce the desired change.

To leverage this, design an environment where the option you'd like people to choose is easier or seen as more attractive, and as a result, is more likely to be chosen.

This still gives people the autonomy to choose from a set of options, but they are nudged into choosing one over the others by how it's presented.

For example, if you wanted employees to sign up for 401(k) matching, you can make it the default setting when they elect benefits so that they would need to choose to opt out if they don't want it.

Microsoft Viva employs AI-based nudges to prompt different behaviors based on things being tracked, such as hours spent in meetings or emails sent outside of working hours.

If the goal is a healthier workforce, the environment has to make health the path of least resistance. Culture follows behavior, and behavior follows design.

Healthy food on-site. Walking paths. Incentives for physical activity. Email configured to respect working hours. And leaders who don't just permit walking meetings — they schedule them.

Strategies for Driving Change Successfully

Framing the Change Effectively

How people perceive a change determines how they interact with it. Leaders can alter adoption simply by how they position it.

Start by establishing the burning platform — why this change, why now — and pair it with a compelling vision of where you're going. Frame it as part of the business strategy, not the flavor of the month.

Then find the shared motivation that unites all stakeholders in the same quest: the organization's purpose, the need to innovate, the cost of standing still. Get that right, and you don't have to push people toward change. They'll feel pulled toward it.

Leading business thinker and bestselling author David Burkus has outlined three frames, or "fights," leaders can leverage to ignite the need to change:

- Frame the change as a revolution against the status quo (for example, "They say X is acceptable, and we refuse to accept that").

- Frame it as an underdog fight—most effective if the industry or a competitor has judged you as not good enough, but you disagree, and this change will help you prove them wrong.

- Frame it as an ally fight—about a stakeholder, a customer, or someone else in the community that the change will serve.

A good example of this is Paul O'Neill, former CEO of Alcoa. He knew he needed to do more with less to address a slipping share price and organizational performance.

O'Neill knew that getting the company to be more efficient and cost-effective by streamlining processes would not motivate his people. He believed rallying employees around something more inspiring—like safety—would. So, O'Neill in "picked a fight" with a common enemy.

Here, the enemy was the industry standard that allowed an "acceptable" amount of risk. O'Neill fought the idea that any risk—any injury—was acceptable and challenged his employees to ensure that there were zero injuries at Alcoa.

He continued to drive home the message that accidents were the enemy, and any time there was an accident, he and the chain of command below him publicly took the blame for failing to prevent the accident. He also told all employees to call him to suggest new safety practices, especially if their managers weren't listening or implementing their ideas.

He set the example again when an accident occurred and an employee attempted to cover it up. That employee was fired two days later. The new focus on transparency around safety numbers and new ways of thinking opened people up to share ideas.

Because O'Neill chose something truly inspiring—like people protecting each other from accidents—he was able to motivate leaders, union reps, and the average employee.

When O'Neill left Alcoa thirteen years later, the company's income had increased fivefold, and its market value increased from $3 billion to $27 billion.

Senior Leadership Alignment and Commitment

To ensure leaders are aware, bought in, and committed to driving the change, a visible senior leader must sponsor and lead the initiative. If leaders aren't role-modeling and rewarding what they want to see, it will not happen.

I recommend holding a session with senior leaders in the beginning to socialize the business case, benefits, vision, and rollout plan. Get their feedback and make any necessary adjustments.

Next, you need to prepare leaders and managers for the change. Depending on how change-savvy they are, it can be helpful to develop a leadership action plan with the actions they will need to take to drive the change—which is more than just sending an email.

It's key that leaders role-model the new behaviors and translate the "why" and how people are expected to change. I recommend providing them with standardized messaging and talking points so that all leaders speak the same language and it comes across as well-thought-out to others.

A good example of leading change this way is when Hans Vestberg first began his tenure as CEO of Verizon. He wanted to transform the company from a seller of smartphones with a service-based culture to an agile organization focused on innovation, so they could harness the potential of 5G.

He knew mandates were not the answer to driving this change, so he took a different approach. He started by visually demonstrating that things were going to be done differently now.

For example, when he would sit in on meetings, he specifically did not sit at the head of the table, demonstrating that the power to speak does not rest only with the CEO. He wanted to convey that power was distributed among teams and networks of the organization and everyone had a role to play.

In creating this new empowering culture, Vestberg took a three-pronged approach focused on leading himself, others, and the organization. The movement leveraged symbolism and recognition to increase the desired behaviors. The top three hundred leaders were given a gold coin to bestow on their team members who were leading by example.

After two weeks, recipients of the coin had to give it to someone else who was living the purpose and culture—and so on and so forth. The beauty of this is that behind each exchange of the coin is a story of someone building human networks, which also produced higher employee engagement scores.

Prepare Managers to Support People

Managers are the lynchpin to change management. They are the closest to their people and have the most direct influence on them. They set the example and are the ones people expect help from in navigating change.

But, there's a big difference between delivering talking points, and internalizing the change. Start by providing managers with the vision, the "why," the impacts on their people, what they'll need to do differently, expectations, and how they and their people will be supported.

Bring them in early to get their feedback on the rollout strategy and plan. Ask them what questions or resistance they expect from their team. Finally, be sure to provide them with plenty of support through training, coaching, messaging, and feedback mechanisms as you roll out.

Design Thinking

Employ journey mapping and personas to understand the people going through the change and how it will impact them. Share the benefits, challenges, and changes to technology, processes, and systems for them specifically.

You also want to articulate exactly what you need each to do differently, down to specific behaviors you want them to start, stop, and continue. You will also want to determine how they will be held accountable and supported.

Leverage Co-Creation to Gain Commitment

True buy-in is achieved when you bring stakeholders, including employees, on the journey. Designing change with them is much more likely to engender commitment, and the solutions are much more likely to solve the real problem because they are closer to the work.

Do this by sharing the reason behind the change and the end state. Then elicit help and ideas by creating mechanisms for idea sharing across all levels of the organization through social platforms, listening sessions, or "action teams" that can formulate ideas and provide input.

You can create smaller employee groups for involvement based on key criteria and targeted questions such as,

"What do you think of the change?" "Why would it work or not work?" "What do you see as the biggest benefits and challenges?" "Is there anything we should remember as we make these changes?"

Overcoming Resistance

If people can't weigh in, they won't buy in. Identify potential resistors and listen to their concerns via focus groups, surveys, and 1-on-1s to surface their hurdles and determine what it would take to overcome them.

Be sure to consider the potential mindset or identity "baggage" they have attached to the current state that needs to be shifted to the future state.

For example, when leading the implementation of a CRM platform, we had to address the fact that asking salespeople to start inputting their contacts and leads into removed control. They were worried that once they shared their data, they could be replaced.

We overcame this by listening to them and helping them understand how, to the contrary, this would streamline the mundane activities and actually free them up to focus their energy on more strategic tasks, relationship-building, and selling—which is the part of the job they enjoyed.

Tap Into Influencers

Harnessing network effects is a valuable method to expedite the achievement of your goals. In many cases, the most influential individuals are not necessarily the most senior but rather those who possess a significant amount of power based on their network connections.

To identify these influential individuals, one strategy is to ask people throughout the organization to name the top three people they trust, seek advice from, or consult with to validate ideas.

Targeted Engagement

Develop a targeted plan to engage everyone (internally and externally) impacted by the change to be sure they get it, understand the impacts, benefits, and expectations of them in the new world, and how they'll be supported.

This plan should include pre-launch, during, and post-launch communication and change activities. Things should be communicated from the audience's perspective, meeting them on their channels and leveraging existing groups, teams, and networks where possible.

It's key to lead with the "what's in it for them" and what they need to know instead of just what the sender wants to say.

It's also important to communicate the message multiple times, in different content forms, across various channels because people access and digest information in different ways at different times and for different purposes.

Design a Series of Launch Events

When introducing a change, it can be helpful to take over the organization's environments (virtual and physical) with murals, posters, swag, laptop screensavers, and app notifications.

When one of my clients launched a sales engagement platform, we created an online hub and app that outlined the change and what it meant to employees, along with a collection of user stories of people bringing the change to life. This also served as a place for people to ask questions and share pain points and other feedback.

Meet them on their channels, provoke discussions, and ensure consistent, clear messaging around the change as part of an ongoing conversation. This helps employees understand their role and empowers them to own it.

Leverage gamification, such as leaderboards, contests, incentives, badges, and other recognition mechanisms to build competition and fun around wins and people demonstrating the right behaviors.

Build a Network of Change Agents

One way to engage groups of stakeholders early and often is to create a change network. A change network provides a structured way to engage influencers, share important information such as accomplishments, challenges, and contingency plans, and solicit feedback.

Change agents are the "boots on the ground" who have the skills and knowledge related to the change and the ability to translate feedback, communicate effectively, and provide advocacy.

A change network may be structured as one group or divided to support project phases, various geographies, or employee levels.

One of my large-scale transformation projects employed a multi-tiered change network that met monthly—first with the leadership change agents, then middle manager agents, and finally with frontline employee agents.

We found that empowering and bringing change agents from different vantage points together to share feedback and help build the solutions led to greater understanding and advocacy from all levels of the organization.

Targeted Enablement

When one of my clients rolled out a new marketing platform, we ditched the typical click-through demo. Instead, the Chief Marketing Officer opened each session by covering the why behind the platform, the benefits to the team, what was expected, and how people would be supported. By leading with context before training, employees could see not just how the tool worked — but how it made their jobs better.

Equally important is a robust hyper-care support model. Think Apple Genius Bar: minimizes friction, builds confidence, and ensures new behaviors actually stick.

Start Small to Collect Quick Wins

Pilots and team-level changes can provide powerful proof points in building team pride and demonstrating efficacy to future participants as they help the movement gain steam.

Collect these stories in 1-on-1s, surveys, focus groups, etc., and leveraging them in talking points and communications about the change.

Sustainability

To see lasting results, you need a solid sustainability plan that goes beyond go-live, encompassing ongoing measurement, comms, feedback, and support. Use what you learn to iterate continuously, stay ahead of obstacles, and keep the initiative aligned with stakeholder needs.

Reinforcement

To make it stick, embed new behaviors into the systems and structures people interact with every day: performance reviews, recognition, onboarding, incentives, learning, and communication. When the organizational infrastructure reinforces the change, it stops being an initiative and becomes the way things are done.

Measurement

Peter Drucker's maxim holds as true for change as it does for anything else: what gets measured, gets managed. Establish KPIs from the start — training completion, platform adoption, awareness, sentiment, and behavior change. These tell you whether the change is landing. But the metric that moves leaders is value realized — the tangible return the organization is seeing as a result.

Feedback

Measurement tells you what's happening — feedback tells you why. Create both active and passive channels for real-time input: pulse surveys, focus groups, Slack channels, open inboxes, 1-on-1s. Surface pain points early, before small friction becomes large resistance.

Building Change Capability Across the Organization

The organizations that thrive don't just manage change — they build it into their DNA. Living in permanent beta means continuously evolving rather than lurching from one disruption to the next.

That starts at the top. Senior leaders must visibly champion transformation and cultivate a psychologically safe culture where experimentation, risk-taking, and learning from failure are not just tolerated — they're expected.

Operationally, an organization-wide dashboard that tracks the status of projects, upcoming changes, and initiatives gives people visibility, enables better planning, and helps prevent change fatigue from setting in.

For organizations serious about scaling this capability, consider appointing a Chief Transformation Officer. A dedicated transformation office — responsible for vetting, implementing, and measuring all organizational change — ensures coordination across business units and integrates every initiative into a coherent, enterprise-wide strategy.

How your organization manages change is a proxy for how it operates overall — and it will make or break the success of any new initiative, technology, or business model.

Over the years, my work across change management, business transformation, and employee experience has revealed the same keys to managing change well: transparency, co-creation, human-centered design, strategic engagement, friction minimization, and working with human nature rather than against it.

Change is not a project with a start and end date. It is the permanent condition of any organization that is alive and growing.

The question is never whether your organization will change — it will, whether you drive it intentionally or it happens to you.

The question is whether you'll build the culture, capabilities, and conditions to make change something your people lean into rather than run from.

Organizations that embed psychological safety, co-creation, and continuous learning as the norm — not the exception — find that transformation becomes self-sustaining. The energy that once leaked out in resistance flows forward instead.

So — now that we've demystified why most change efforts fail and explored what works instead — how will you use these insights to unlock the full potential of your people and your organization?

CONCLUSION

As we emerge from the past few years, one thing is clear: we're "not in Kansas anymore."

Our ways of working have grown increasingly outdated for decades, and the relationship between companies and employees is undergoing a profound redefinition.

Even if we wanted to go "back to normal," there's no "back" to go back to. The world has changed. We've changed. And so what do we do? We evolve.

In one of his recent CEO letters, BlackRock CEO Larry Fink reminds us that the essence of capitalism lies in constant reinvention.

As we've entered into what McKinsey calls the era of perpetual upheaval, how organizations navigate these headwinds and shifts will determine their survival.

Organizations can no longer afford to view employee thriving and business outcomes at the expense of each other.

Instead, a new understanding is emerging of the symbiotic, and even causal, relationship between the two. Countless studies and real-world applications consistently demonstrate that when employees flourish, the organization prospers.

Leaders need to be asking themselves whether they are creating an environment that helps them win in the talent pool, because that is what will help them win in the marketplace.

To create what Warren Buffett refers to as a "moat," or a sustainable competitive advantage, companies must cultivate environments that prioritize the changing needs and expectations of the modern, human workforce. Failure to do so risks making the organization less appealing, less productive, and ultimately less successful.

On the other hand, organizations that embrace this shift will tap into a wellspring of motivation, innovation, exceptional performance, and loyalty, which translate directly into business outcomes.

We started this journey by looking at the challenges facing organizations today, and how old mindsets and ways of working hinder the performance of employees, as well as the organization.

Through in-depth research, juicy stories, and practical solutions, we've highlighted various strategic levers you can pull to flip the script and create the conditions for your people to be the most productive, engaged, and high-performing version of themselves in this new world.

As leaders and changemakers, you play a key role in this pivotal moment, to create the future of work.

One where people aren't burned out, disengaged, disconnected, quietly quitting, languishing, or otherwise leading "lives of quiet desperation."

Now that I've armed you with the tools to transform your organization into one that enriches lives and fuels exceptional performance, how will you reimagine work and steward its evolution?

The organizations that will thrive in the coming decades are not necessarily the ones with the most capital, the best technology, or the cleverest strategy.

They will be the ones that have figured out how to unlock the full potential of their people—by creating environments where human beings can do the best work of their lives.

The Medici didn't just fund art. They created the conditions for a renaissance.

That's what the best organizations do: they don't just employ people—they help them flourish. And when people flourish, the business does too. That is The Flourishing Effect.

How to Get Started

You can get started by joining me and our community of unapologetic changemakers making moves to make work better:

Connect with me on LinkedIn, where you can sign up for The Flourishing Effect newsletter and continue the discussion. I would love to hear what resonates with you, how you are implementing the ideas and strategies, and other best practices you discover.

Head to my website www.tonillemiller.com where you can find additional media, tools, and other exclusive content.

Provide a quick review on Amazon with the takeaway you found most helpful from the book. This helps other people in the community find the book too.

REFERENCES

This book draws on extensive research—hundreds of citations.

To honor my value of environmental stewardship, I've made the complete bibliography available online rather than printing additional pages in every book.

Access all references at:

www.tonillemiller.com/tfereferences.

www.ingramcontent.com/pod-product-compliance
Lightning Source LLC
Chambersburg PA
CBHW070104030426
42335CB00016B/1997